I Could Go On...

I Could
Go On...

Unpublished Letters to
The Daily Telegraph

EDITED BY
IAIN HOLLINGSHEAD

First published in Great Britain
2010 by Aurum Press Ltd
74–77 White Lion Street
London N1 9PF
www.aurumpress.co.uk

This edition published in 2013 by Aurum Press Ltd

A catalogue record for this book is available from the
British Library.

ISBN: 978 1 78131 240 7

10 9 8 7 6 5 4 3 2 1
2017 2016 2015 2014 2013

Designed and typeset in Mrs Eaves by
Roger Hammond, Bluegum
Printed and bound by CPI Group (UK) Ltd,
Croydon, CR0 4YY

SIR — One of the presents my wife gave me on Christmas Day was *Am I Alone in Thinking...? Unpublished Letters to The Daily Telegraph.*

I take great comfort in the fact that, despite these troubled and uncertain times, the Great British sense of humour is still very much alive and well. I should like it to be known that, while reading the book, I almost wet myself on at least three separate occasions.

Bruce Chalmers
Goring by Sea, West Sussex

SIR — I have a big dilemma — do I hope that my letters are not printed and that they might appear in the book of unpublished letters at the end of the year, or do I go for the glory of seeing my letter in print in the newspaper?

The book, of course, will make a better Christmas present if one of my letters is included.

If all fails, I can only hope that one of my photos will appear on the BBC weather programme.

Veronica Bliss
Compton, Hampshire

SIR — Seeing my wife's previously unpublished letter in *Am I Alone in Thinking...?*, a lifelong friend sent her a text message: "One up on old man — him only in paper, you in book."

"Not so," responded Anne. "Him in book too!" Has any other couple managed the double?

Robert Warner
Aston, Oxfordshire

SIR — I have put up with my husband's rants staring at me from your letter pages. However, it really is too much to discover on reaching page 104 of *Am I Alone in Thinking...?* that our dog also holds trenchant views on life.

By way of punishment I am withholding treats and walkies. I shall probably do the same with the dog.

Kate Fell
Flintham, Nottinghamshire

SIR — Is it just me, or am I alone in thinking that I could go on?

Mike Comiskey
London SE5

CONTENTS

INTRODUCTION

Even after working on *The Daily Telegraph's* letters desk for a while, one can rarely predict which topics will get our admirable readers going next. One moment it's the defence of the realm, the state of the NHS and the challenge of alternative energy sources. The next, they're sharing their thoughts on the best headgear for middle-aged drivers of sports cars, or the kindest ways to prevent garden birds flying into French windows.

One of the most enjoyable – and longest-running – correspondences this year concerned our readers' recollections of their school reports. It started from nowhere and went on for several weeks, including such gems as: "When the workers of the world unite it would be presumptuous of Dewhurst to include himself among their number"; "Unlike the poor, Graham is seldom with us"; and "The improvement in his handwriting has revealed his inability to spell".

The only thing of which one can be certain on the letters desk is that the correspondence will keep pouring in. Modern technology has changed the way in which readers interact with their newspaper, but it hasn't hastened the death of the letters page. Quite the opposite, in fact. Of the 700 letters we receive on average each day – a huge increase on the pre-internet era – at least 500 arrive by email. "Letters to the Editor" offer a coherent, carefully edited space – a kind of daily competition, if you will

– that exhibits the best of what our readers are thinking. They are seldom shy of sharing these thoughts, writing from their offices, from holiday – even, in one instance, from the bath. One correspondent suggested that we run a separate letters page for emails sent after pub closing time.

Well, we haven't decided to do that – yet. But last year I had the idea of collating some of the best unpublished letters into a book for the first time. Some of them hadn't made the newspaper as they arrived too late and the news agenda had moved on, or they addressed an interesting topic which didn't quite fit with the rest of the day's selection (we only have space to publish around 20). Sometimes, they were too whimsical, or indeed too risqué, for a serious daily newspaper. Sometimes, frankly, they were completely and utterly (and wonderfully) mad.

Am I Alone in Thinking...? proved to be a surprise Christmas bestseller, appealing to both old and new readers. Happily, the answer to the book's semi-rhetorical title was a resounding "No". Jennifer Latham, writing from Wedmore in Somerset, spoke for many in her pleasure at discovering "what a cheeky, irreverent lot fellow readers are... Greed, envy, lust, revolution, nuttiness, political incorrectness – brilliant reading, all." Katrin Ziegler, an English teacher in Ottweiler, Germany, said that she had used the book in lessons with her 16-year-old pupils. We printed a few of these letters in the paper, delighting in the irony of

publishing letters about previously unpublished
letters, which had now been published.

Initially, I was reluctant to attempt a follow-up
edition. I had begun working in other parts of the
newspaper; producing a completely new book would
mean another year of skimming through 5,000
emails a week. Would it be as fun as the first one?
Would it be as popular? Our readers might not be
alone in thinking the way they do, but could they —
in another phrase beloved of regular correspondents
— "go on and on"?

Fortunately, the answer this time is an equally
decisive "Yes". To an extent, we have been lucky with
events this past year (these letters were collated
between October 2009 and August 2010): the
departures of Gordon Brown, Tony Hayward and
Jonathan Ross have provided much fodder for our
letter-writers' cannons; as has the arrival of Chris
Evans. Popular chapters on politics, television,
foreign affairs, crime and punishment, and domestic
dystopia return in entirely new forms, while in a
change from *Am I Alone in Thinking...?* there is an entire
section on sport this time round, sprinkled with
observations on the elasticity of John Terry's and
Tiger Woods's trousers, Andy Murray's facial hair
and, of course, the vuvuzela.

Elsewhere, fans of M, the correspondent who
believes himself to be the head of MI6, issuing
orders from an internet café in Bristol, will be
delighted to see that his thoughts on world events

pop up again. My favourite is his memo suggesting that Tony Blair – who vies here with Ed Balls, Peter Mandelson and Harriet Harman for being the target of the most hilarious bile – played a part in the fox attack on two young twins.

It has certainly been an eventful year. But our wonderful correspondents, as quick and as able to turn their hand to letters about geopolitics as their gardens, have never been constrained by the vagaries of the news cycle. I should have had more faith in them when I was doubtful about repeating the task of editing a new collection of unpublished letters. It has been more fun than I could have imagined. To them, my grateful thanks – as well as to Christopher Howse, the letters editor; Dorothy, Matilda and Alex on the letters desk; Matt Pritchett; Caroline Buckland; Richard Preston; and everyone at Aurum.

I could go on... but I will leave that to our readers who *really* can. I hope I'm not alone in thinking they have been on cracking form of late.

Iain Hollingshead
The Daily Telegraph
London SW1
August 2010

A YEAR IS
A LONG TIME
IN POLITICS

NEW YEAR'S RESOLUTIONS
2010

SIR – All I want for 2010 is a resounding kicking for Labour candidates and an end to the DFS sale.

Peter Bradshaw
Liverpool

SIR – Dear Lord, I know that I don't talk to you that much, but I note that you have recently taken away my favourite actor, Patrick Swayze, my favourite actress, Farrah Fawcett, my favourite musician, Michael Jackson, and my favourite cricketer, Alec Bedser.

I just wanted to let you know that my favourite prime minister is Gordon Brown. Amen.

David Say
St Ives, Cornwall

SIR – Who will rid me of this turbulent Prime Minister? Well, it worked for Henry II.

Happy New Year.

Andreas Wright
Bessines sur Gartempe, France

SIR – Press releases on Gordon Brown's love of bananas and his favourite biscuits demonstrate the infantilisation of Downing Street. Can this really be the same office that once ruled an Empire?

Andrew M. Rosemarine MA (Juris) BCL (Oxon)
LicSpecDrEur (ULB)
Salford, West Midlands

SIR – In his Christmas message the Prime Minister told troops in Afghanistan that this year had tested their resolve more than any other.

In my Christmas message to Gordon Brown I can tell him that he and his Government have had a similar effect upon me.

Lieutenant Colonel Richard King-Evans
Hambye, France

CARRY ON UP THE BERCOWS

SIR – With the revelations about their private lives, it is about time John Bercow and his wife starred in a new film called *Carry on Commons*.

It would have all the ingredients for success: a beautiful leggy blonde and a sexually frustrated little man brought together by a desire to make their fortune.

Ted Shorter
Hildenborough, Kent

SIR — Sally Bercow, the wife of the speaker, admits to a drunken ladette past by drinking a whole bottle of wine a day, maybe even two. SHOCK! HORROR!

Dear Sally, a word to the wise: consuming two bottles of wine a day does not make you a drunk; it makes you a passable companion for dinner. Two bottles of vodka, you're getting there. Two bottles of vodka and bottles of wine for chasers, you're definitely getting there.

You were not a ladette, dear Sally. You were a poor wino, and barely an accomplished one at that.

Albert Roy
London E3

EVER-CLOSER DISUNION

SIR — At last, with the appointments of Herman Van Rompuy and Baroness Ashton, the EU has political leaders who can sit around the table with other similarly elected world leaders: Robert Mugabe (Zimbabwe), Kim Il-Sung (North Korea), Than Shwe (Myanmar) and Gordon Brown (European Western Outpost, formerly Britain).

Colin Mardell
Holbeach, Lincolnshire

SIR – So Baroness Ashton is "proud of being a woman". I have turned that claim upside down and back to front but I still cannot make head nor tail of it. Will she next be telling us that she is proud of having two hands and one nose?

Robert Henderson
London NW1

SIR – Tintin and Mrs Tiggy-Winkle would command more respect on the world stage.

Brian Mahony
Pimperne, Dorset

SIR – Can I express my sincere thanks to those who have taken the two EC posts. I had become seriously concerned that my own name, unknown to millions, was slowly moving up the list of candidates.

Stuart Jamieson
Chorley, Lancashire

SIR – I do not know what all the fuss is about Van Rompuy and Baroness Ashton; I have been living in an undemocratic tyrannical autocracy since the day I married my wife.

Iain McKie
Totland Bay, Isle of Wight

TONY BLAIR'S
SECOND COMING

SIR — My wife was shocked when she saw Tony Blair's perma-tanned second coming on television yesterday. Her first words were: "The future's bright, the poodle's orange."

N.B.

SIR — I don't believe you should judge a man by the colour of his skin, but in the case of Tony Blair I'll make an exception.

Ralph Berry
Stratford-upon-Avon, Warwickshire

SIR — I used to be quite proud of being a member of the human race until I heard Tony Blair's evidence at the Chilcot inquiry.

And this is written before I have heard it.

John Porter
Parkstone, Dorset

SIR — Is it my imagination or has the walk of George W. Bush been passed, like a baton, to Tony Blair and to Gordon Brown? Now even David Cameron appears to have adopted the same gait — something like the way wrestlers approach the ring.

Or is it just that they all suffer from prickly heat of the armpits?

Jim King
St Ives, Cambridgeshire

SIR – Tony Blair equals New Labour equals Nouveau Riche.

Douglas Linington
Ramsey, Cambridgeshire

SIR – Anyone feeling slightly envious on learning the extent of Tony Blair's wealth should console themselves by remembering that he's married to Cherie.

Lawrence Fraser
Elgin, Moray

FOOT NOTE IN HISTORY

SIR – During a discussion about the life and principles of the late Michael Foot, one of my Year 8 students asked: "If he was so left wing, why was he in the Labour Party?"

O tempora! O mores!

Martin Roberts
Oxford

SIR – Michael Foot was truly a Leg-end in his own lifetime.

David Hartridge
Groby, Leicestershire

SIR – Somewhat tasteless I suppose, but I've always anticipated the headline, "Foot kicks the bucket".

Pamela Savery
London NW4

ROYAL ROCKS AND SHOCKS

SIR – Andrew Marr to interview the Queen? Never. Never. Never. He would shout at her, interrupt her and never let her complete an answer.

She is one of the rocks on which this country rests. We do not want this curmudgeon confronting the Queen. Please, Mr Marr, go back to Scotland and stay there.

B.H. Jackson
Sheffield

SIR – What to do with all the wind farms? Easy: adjust the wiring, point them all south-west, set the turbine blades to coarse pitch and gently cruise the British Isles off to the Bay of Biscay.

Unfortunately, during this procedure Scotland might break off because of the Great Glen. This loss is amply compensated by freedom from the risk of bagpipes.

Arthur W.J.G. Ord-Hume
Guildford, Surrey

SIR – Could someone please explain why the activities of the Duke of York as "Special Representative for International Trade and Investment" continue to be written up in the Court Circular? These activities are merely a way of keeping Prince Andrew occupied; they are not royal duties.

Jeremy Parr
Suckley, Worcestershire

SIR – I have a soft spot for Sarah Ferguson; my dream girl looked like her and she reminds me of a boisterous Labrador, my favourite breed of dog.

Mark Taha
London SE26

CULLING POLITICIANS

SIR – Your headline "Tory plans to cull MPs" raised my hopes until I realised that it only referred to reducing the number of parliamentary seats, and not to the actual culling of MPs, which would get my vote every time.

Steve Cattell
Hougham, Lincolnshire

SIR – I have no objection to "castrating" Parliament providing we excise Ed Balls in the process.

John Harvey
Wellow, Nottinghamshire

SIR – Disgraced Conservative MP David Curry observes that "if a guillotine were erected on Parliament Square, the public would fight for tickets to watch the blood flow".

Au contraire, Monsieur Curry; I would queue patiently for my ticket, safe in the knowledge that there are plenty of candidates for the chop. The wait would simply enhance my enjoyment of the dénouement.

Anthony Lord
Thornton-Cleveleys, Lancashire

SIR – Nick Clegg states that his house belongs to everyone. So that makes it a timeshare property. May I have the first two weeks in August, please?

B.J.
London SE15

SIR – One good thing to come out of our MPs' financial shenanigans is that when your quick crossword setter asks the clue "redact" we all know the answer.

Frank Dike
Salwayash, Dorset

BULLY FOR GORDON

SIR – Given the stories about the alleged shenanigans in Number 10 over the weekend, I was looking forward to Matt's cartoon on the front page. Alas, nothing. Has Gordon Brown's bullying extended its focus?

Roy Hembrough
Disley, Cheshire

SIR – Gordon Brown admits to throwing things, but says he has never hit anyone. So it seems that along with all his other failings, he is a rotten shot.

Can the man get nothing right?

Alan Dyer-Perry
North Elmham, Norfolk

SIR – Should Labour's election slogan not be, "A future fair for all – or we'll throw a printer at you"?

Eldon Sandys
Pyrford, Surrey

SIR – Why the wait? I want my fair sooner rather than later, and it had better be big, like Thorpe Park. Otherwise I'm not playing.

Kate Battersby
Cheapside, Berkshire

SIR – Gordon Brown's smile – could it be wind?

M.H.
Suffolk

AND WE'RE OFF...

SIR – May I suggest you publish your election coverage in the same way as your business and sports coverage – in throwaway sections.

Martin Yirrell
Hemel Hempstead, Hertfordshire

SIR – After we have read *The Daily Telegraph* front to back, I use the paper to line the bottom of our parrots' four cages, with the Labour candidates face up.

Daphne MacOwan
Ramsey, Isle of Man

SIR – I bought a red rose for my buttonhole to celebrate St George's Day. I was not afraid of being thought a racist; however, I was terrified of being mistaken as a Labour supporter.

Philip Samengo-Turner
London SW11

SIR – Frequently in recent days, members of the televised media have been debating into whose hands will be given "the keys to Number 10".

To my knowledge, there are no keyholes in the front door of 10 Downing Street as it is always opened from the inside. In light of this, should the first job of the Prime Minister be to seek precise advice from the electorate as to which opening he should insert said keys into?

If it is Gordon Brown, I have at least one suggestion, trusting that the keyring is suitably large.

Douglas Knight
Chipperfield, Hertfordshire

TV'S DESPICABLE NICK CLEGG

SIR – I for one will not be voting for a man who so despises the electorate that he stands before them with his hands in his pockets, as did Nick Clegg the other night during the televised debate. Can we now expect him to address us all as *Mate*?

Lieutenant Commander Philip Barber (retd)
Norton Juxta Twycross, Leicestershire

SIR — Why all the fuss about Nick Clegg's performance on the television debate? By his own admission he managed to sweet-talk at least 30 women into his bed.

Sandra Mitchell
London W13

SIR — At last the answer as to how to re-invigorate *Strictly Come Dancing*. A new face, a new personality, not camera-shy, untried but likeable… Nick Clegg has displayed all the qualities to be a first-class TV presenter and could even work without the help of an autocue.

Watch your back, Bruce.

Jean Ratcliff
Barnet, Hertfordshire

SIR — Please help a confused voter, who did not see the much-talked-about televised debate. Is Mr N. Clegg the same Mr N. Clegg who was so muddled in *Last of the Summer Wine*?

R.A. Last
South Croydon, Surrey

SIR –

"I'm bigger than Jesus!".
("Nick" Clegg, after just one TV "Debate")
We've heard that one before:
John Lennon.
And it ended in DISASTER.
A lawful, free and fair election
Requires the "damping down" of any "Boy Cult"
Which seems to have "taken hold".
Because Clegg's "The Future Son-In-Law"
Nobody knows ANYTHING about.
That's all.
cc MI5
Etc.

M

WHEN GORDON MET GILLIAN

SIR – If I had been in Gordon Brown's shoes
when leaving Gillian Duffy's house to face the media
I would have hung my head in shame for what I
had said, not stood there smiling like a hyena
with diarrhoea.

J.R.
Scarborough, North Yorkshire

SIR – I would think that Gillian Duffy, 65, is probably more annoyed at being described as "elderly" than a "bigot".

Andrew J. Morrison (64 yrs and 355 days)
Faveraye-Machelles, France

SIR – I was hugely reassured by Gordon Brown's gaffe. He does stupid things, just like I do. It highlights the folly of spending hundreds of thousands of pounds charging around the country trying to convince the British people that in no way are you actually a complete penguin.

David S-P
India

HOVERING PENCIL SYNDROME

SIR – I knew a professor at college who had an unusual method of deciding which party would obtain his vote. He acquired copies of all the manifestos and proceeded to mark them as one would an essay. He subsequently voted for the party whose manifesto contained the fewest grammatical errors.

Harry Drummond
Midhurst, West Sussex

SIR – Totally ignored by a Conservative government or "reached out to" by a Labour one? Hmm, let me think...

Nick Luke
Bath

SIR – I wonder how many of your readers are like me in wishing the leaders of our main parties were Samantha Cameron, Sarah Brown and Miriam Clegg.

Iris J.L. Wells
York

SIR – Simon Heffer for Prime Minister.

Stephen Butterton
St Leonard's-on-Sea, East Sussex

SIR – Am I alone in thinking that the biggest worry is that, after the General Election, we'll still just be left with a bunch of politicians running the country?

A.G.
Maidstone, Kent

THE LONG GOODBYE

SIR — Why, when I contemplate the physical removal of Gordon Brown from 10 Downing Street, am I put in mind of my wife trying to put our cat into its carrier for a trip to the vet?

Ian Bruce
Hockley Heath, West Midlands

SIR — The front door of 10 Downing Street has been seen on television a great deal lately. The black gloss paintwork is exemplary. But isn't it irritating that the O of the number 10 is skew-whiff?

I hope that whoever's the next prime minister makes putting this straight a priority.

David Wagstaff
Coventry

SIR — Will someone now finish the job and drive a wooden stake through the heart of Lord Mandelson?

Jeremy R.G. Bloomfield
East Stour, Dorset

OH HAPPY DAY

SIR – I noticed that Gordon Brown took very slow steps back into Downing Street after making his final statement as Prime Minister. I wasn't sure whether he looked more like an undertaker walking in front of a hearse or someone suffering an acute attack of piles.

It would be wonderful if it could be arranged for a gospel choir to be positioned outside when he leaves office to sing "Oh Happy Day".

Richard Martin
Epsom, Surrey

SIR – I am taking a prime ministerial and statesman-like decision to resign from my tennis club, because I cannot win.

Jeff Wilcox-Smith
Wing, Leicestershire

SIR – What a relief not to have numerous Scottish accents telling us what to do.

John Reeves
Fairseat, Kent

SIR – The Labour Party has committed
TREASON and should be indicted accordingly.
The economic mess in which we find ourselves has
not occurred by accident. It has been carefully and
systematically planned for a very long time.

In English Law, High Treason was punishable by
being hanged, drawn and quartered. Women were
simply burnt at the stake.

Peter Stocken
Frimley, Surrey

WHERE'S WALLY?

SIR – Where's Wally (oh, I mean Gordon)?

Jo Parker
Warwick

SIR – I have just been reading Dr Seuss's seminal
work, *Hop on Pop*, to my 18-month-old son, and came
across the following: "Pup up, Brown down, pup is
down. Where is Brown? Where is Brown? There is
Brown! Mr Brown is out of town."

Was the great doctor's PhD in psephology?

Alice Rose
London W12

SIR — I just saw Mr Brown sidle into South Queensferry Airport and catch the 4.30am flight to Mogadishu. He has, I gather, just bought a whelk stall there.

Tony Horsfield
Angmering, West Sussex

SIR — I would like to thank the Conservatives and Liberals for curing me of my health problems. As a result of the disappearance of the Brown, Mandelson and Campbell virus my projectile vomiting has completely cleared up.

David Lawson
Chobham, Surrey

THE NICK 'N' DAVE SHOW

SIR – Am I alone in thinking that Nick and Dave were going to walk away from their first Downing Street press conference holding hands?

John Ward
Ashampstead, Berkshire

SIR – The Dave and Nick partnership appears to be on track. However, if one exchanges the first letter of their names the omens might not bode so well for the future.

Brian Smith
Chelmsford, Essex

SIR – You can say what you want about the Tories, but at least they know how to organise some decent summer weather.

Jonathan L. Kelly
Yatton, North Somerset

SIR – Liberals have tramped the way to hell from the beginning, making me believe that the first Liberal might have been the Serpent in the Garden of Eden: "Go on Eve, have a bite; you deserve it."

R. Dayton Lewis
Cowes, Isle of Wight

SIR –
 "Watch"
 "10 Downing Street"
 Because it seems to be FULL of a lot of IMMATURE people
 at the moment.
 "Virgins".
 "Top Table Virgins"
 All so terribly excited about "Being At The Top".
 WHERE "POWER" IS.
 Like it's f****** 'Freshers' Fair.
 All "Doing The Okey Cokey".
 With every "David Laws".
 Around the garden of "10 Downing Street".
 While the Russians THINK.
 And the Irish DRINK.
 And "plot".
 YOU HAVE BEEN WARNED.
 About "Silly People".
 In the "SILLY SEASON"
 cc "MI7"

 M

TACKLING THE CORDUROY DEFICIT

SIR – As David Cameron, the Prime Minister, struggles to save money, he could well look at Sport, Culture, Art and Music (SCAM), which have drained the British taxpayer of some £560 million every year for the last 20 years, to the benefit of no one except the thousands of luvvies that this money keeps in fine corduroy style.

Surely they could do just as well down a coal mine, if only to marvel at the wonder of it all.

Malcolm Parkin
Kinnesswood, Kinross

SIR – If we charged for all the terrorist training carried out in Britain it could relieve the country of its debt within a year or so.

A.P.
Warwick

SIR – Maybe the economic position won't be so bad after Tony Blair has paid the full amount of tax on his £12 million earnings.

David Whiteley
London SW15

SIR – I may be guilty of treason and be condemned to years in a damp, dark dungeon, but it does occur to me that we could save a few quid if the Queen performed the State Opening of Parliament by car with just a couple of outriders.

The content of the speech itself could be confined to: "Right, you lot, get on with it and sort the mess out."

I love all the pageantry, but it must come hellish expensive.

Gavin Inglis
Westcliff-on-Sea, Essex

SIR – The national debt could be cleared in a week if a £100 fixed penalty was applied to anyone parking on the pavement.

Jim Alexander
Lichfield, Staffordshire

SIR – If Michael O'Leary were to hold the post of Prime Minister, we would all be in for a tax rebate by the end of his first term.

H. Morris
Ware, Hertfordshire

SIR – May I suggest the introduction of a tax for heavy users of exclamation marks? It is a problem that seems to have blown up under the last government while Gordon Brown had his eye on other things.

I'm fed up with reading lots of them, in places where they clearly don't belong. A pay-as-you-exclaim fee should be added to mobile phone charges. Then the melodramatic culprits might think twice before they spoil their text with unsightly blemishes.

Judd Flogdell
Middle Barton, Oxfordshire

SIR – I have to admit that I misjudged the strength of feeling by public-sector workers against the cuts – right up to the moment I tried to reduce by 25 per cent the amount of housekeeping money I give to my wife.

Hugh Stewart-Smith
London E11

SAMCAM AND DAVE THE
ODD-JOB MAN

SIR — While it is welcome to see the vivacious
Samantha Cameron and read about her support for
her husband, why does she refer to him as "Dave"?
This is so degrading. It makes him sound like an
odd-job man. We don't hear about Nic Sarkozy or
Ange Merkel.

David Hartridge
Groby, Leicestershire

SIR — So David Cameron has "tried" to stop his
daughter Nancy listening to what he has decided is
unsuitable music. "Tried"? What is this "tried"?
Isn't she six years old? Couldn't he just tell her
that she is not allowed to listen to it? Who is in
control here?

P.D.
Worthing, Sussex

MAYDAY, GIDEON

SIR – While I am generally in favour of people learning on the job, I think it mindless to entrust the post of Chancellor of the Exchequer to George Osborne, whose sole qualification for the role appears to be his boundless self-confidence.
One might as well ask Gideon to try to land a fully-laden jumbo jet with three engines out and running low on fuel.

Andy Smith
Kingston-upon-Thames, Surrey

SILLY LITTLE BALLS

SIR – Ed Balls tell us that he "wants to be himself". What was he before? A cardboard cut-out? Or just morally and intellectually bankrupt?
Silly little man.
Unfit for any purpose, I would suggest.

David Bird
Esher, Surrey

SIR – I have just listened to a debate on Jeremy
Vine's programme. Ed Balls, now Shadow Education
Secretary, was discussing what he referred to as
"Skoows" and "Eyd yoo kayshun".

For my grandchildren's sake, Coalition, please
hang on in there.

Ray Bather
Spartylea, Northumberland

BUTTONED-UP MILIBAND

SIR – If anyone is unsure whether or not to vote for
David Miliband, I would draw their attention to the
photo of him in *The Daily Telegraph* wearing a
two-buttoned suit with both buttons done up.

Patrick Wroe
Felixstowe, Suffolk

SIR – I am deeply puzzled by the thing on David
Miliband's upper lip. Is it a) a piece of dead rabbit;
b) a fugitive moustache; or c) is he just too young
to shave?

Victoria Knollys
Salisbury, Wiltshire

THE THIRD MAN(DELSON)

SIR – Lord Mandelson's choice of title is telling.
Am I alone in thinking that, even with all the damage
the previous holder of this epithet did to our
country, it is an insult to Kim Philby?

Donald Marsh
London N19

SIR – If a plagiarised title is considered acceptable,
would not *Diary of a Nobody* be more apt?

Roger Manning
Weybridge, Surrey

SIR – In a calculated snub to Tony Blair, I intend
to ignore Peter Mandelson's memoirs before I
ignore his.

Gordon Brown
Grassington, North Yorkshire

LORD OF THE PIES

SIR – Surely John Prescott's new title should be Lord Prescott of Pyestock?

C.H.P. Piff
Downley, Buckinghamshire

SIR – Am I the only one disappointed that John Prescott didn't choose a more appropriate title, say Baron Ay-Up.

I.C.
Wirral

SIR – Is it just me, or did anyone else notice that we never once saw Paul the Octopus and Baron Prescott of Kingston-upon-Hull together in the same shot?

Huw Beynon
Llandeilo, Carmarthenshire

DOMESTIC
DYSTOPIA

YOU REALLY
SHOULDN'T HAVE...

SIR – On our first wedding anniversary my husband disappeared to the village and I imagined he had gone to buy me a present. He eventually returned with a hosepipe and a car-cleaning brush.

Subsequent anniversaries have brought nothing so I suppose I should be grateful for small mercies. In other ways he is kind and helpful about the house, and we have been married for 57 years.

Sally Davies
Bramhall, Cheshire

SIR – Some years ago my husband bought me an orange, electric, concrete mixer for our wedding anniversary. A friend asked: "Did you not mind him buying you that?"

I said no; until then I had been mixing the concrete by hand.

Shonagh Finnan
West Horsley, Surrey

SIR — Several years ago my husband gave me a second-hand wicker laundry basket as a Christmas present; he is still trying to pry it off his head.

Carole Waters
Chelmorton, Derbyshire

SIR — It is all very well spoiling wives by buying them a rotary clothes line for Christmas, but does it stop there? The next thing you know, they will want the accessories: a new washing machine, a new set of clothes pegs, a new washing basket. The list could be endless.

Nairn Lawson
Portbury, Somerset

SIR — I read that Argentina has, at last, legalised same-sex marriages. This pleases me: at this rate of progress, I shall soon be allowed to marry my neighbour's motorbike.

Kevin Hutchinson
Maulden, Bedfordshire

SIR — My attempt to send a Valentine to myself to make my husband jealous was a waste of money. The roses were wilted and of very poor quality, and my beloved did not notice them anyway until I pointed them out.

Rather sad, really.

P.P.
Blewbury, Oxfordshire

SIR — My husband's wife-listening app seems to have broken. Is this to be expected after more than 20 years of marriage?

L.F.
Farnham, Surrey

SIR — I have decided that the best way to get my husband of nearly 47 years to take notice of me at the breakfast table would be to have whatever it is that I wish to say to him published on your letters page.

Wendy Breese
Lingfield, Surrey

BATHING WITH BLONDES

SIR – Perusing the papers today, I was struck by the number of advertisements for walk-in baths, each of which featured an attractive blonde of around 42, pictured either entering or leaving the bath in a swimsuit via the side door.

Is there any particular reason for this age group of blonde ladies requiring walk-in baths? I suspect it may be related to wine but perhaps I have missed something.

Robert Hill
Irby, Wirral

SIR – If I tried balancing my drink on the side of the bath, as suggested by one of your correspondents, I would probably end up with coq au vin.

Michael Talamo
Carshalton, Surrey

SIR – One of my great pleasures in life is daydreaming in a warm, scented bath with my Burmese cat purring contentedly on the edge, while my loyal spaniel sits on a stool, keeping a drowsy, watchful eye over me.

Sometimes I ask my wife to join us.

James Logan
Portstewart, Co. Londonderry

SIR – What more could you want in a bath, one of your correspondent asks. Answer: Rachel Stevens.

Andrew Holgate
Woodley, Cheshire

HOLY DISHWATER

SIR – One incontrovertible proof of the existence of God is that He made sweetcorn kernels exactly the right size to become trapped under the heating elements of dishwashers. He may be largely ignored, but He is still here, gently chiding us.

Graham Masterton
Tadworth Park, Surrey

SIR – Has anyone else noticed that, despite global warming, lavatory seats seem to be getting colder?

Steve Revill
Nottingham

SIR – As a nation of tea drinkers must we tolerate the flooding of the tea tray every time we pour from modern teapot spouts?

Angela Purdon
Coate, Wiltshire

SIR — I wonder if any of your readers can close a bottle of Lea and Perrins without splattering themselves?

Ruth Fisher
Ashirk, Selkirkshire

SIR — What is the best way to eat a ripe peach, pear or nectarine? During the summer my *Daily Telegraph* is saturated with juice dribbled from my chin.

W.E. Leaver
Lot et Garonne, France

SIR — I wonder if any of your readers share my annoyance at so many modern gadgets which constantly beep at you.

If it's not the microwave oven, it's one's mobile phone or computer. We now have a fridge, an oven and a dishwasher that all beep at you if you leave the door open, and even a kettle that beeps when it's boiled the water. Why?

And if that isn't enough, when you leave the house and get in the car, you are assaulted with all manner of beeps and bongs if, God forbid, you do something wrong, reverse or forget to replenish some vital fluid.

When will it all end?

Philip Urlwin-Smith
Chobham, Surrey

SIR – Am I alone in having a garden which is six feet longer than my strimmer lead?

William Miller
Northampton

SIR – A friend of mine has four apple trees in his garden, which he refers to as "the apple trees in my garden". Another friend also has four apple trees, which he slightly pompously refers to as "my orchard". Is there a definitive number of apple trees that one has to have before one can officially call it an orchard?

Graham Phillips
Hope Cove, Devon

FOXY FUN

SIR – Some years ago a fox regularly visited our garden, regurgitating small, partially digested creatures on the patio. My wife claimed to have a remedy. Duly instructed, I stood in the corner of our garden at dusk and discreetly and copiously urinated on the garden wall.

There have been no sightings of foxes since.

Kenneth Allen
Riddlesden, West Yorkshire

SIR – Following the widely reported fox attack, could I propose some knee-jerk legislation: fox hunting on the national curriculum; compulsory beagling for under-fives; and a stag-hunting NVQ.

Jonathan H. Fulford
Bosham, West Sussex

SIR – Not wishing to trivialise the distressing attack by a fox on two infants, but I was bitten on the knee three weeks ago by a sheep while I was having my lunch at a Peak District beauty spot.

A mugshot is available of the perpetrator if a line-up can be formed.

Eva A. Krystek
Hale, Cheshire

SIR –

IGNORE.

This so-called "Savage Fox" case.

Apparently attacking twins.

Because amazingly, it's "Tony" Blair.

Who seems to have become some sort of

"Al" Capone.

Yeah, mate.

Foxes never climb the stairs like.

But in this case.

It has.

'Cos that's what you want us to say.

Right, "Tony"?

cc MI7

M

NANNY DOES NOT KNOW BEST

SIR – Now that the Government is to spend £2.7 million on a campaign to persuade me to lose my non-existent spare tyre, I have decided to renounce my regular walks on the Malvern Hills and take a far greater interest in red wine and pies.

Mike Redman
Malvern, Worcestershire

SIR – Those nannying "experts" who constantly exhort people to reduce their alcohol consumption should realise that some excessive drinkers, myself included, indulge their habit in the hope that it might bring their miserable lives to a premature conclusion. Such a protracted form of attempted suicide, while not guaranteed to be successful, does at least provide some comfort.

T.L.
Lancashire

THE DRINKING CLASSES

SIR – If Gordon Brown really wants to know which class people belong to, all he has to do is to ask where their milk comes from.

Lower class: Supermarket.

Middle class: Door step, via milkman.

Upper class: No idea, old boy.

We can guess which class Gordon is in.

Chaz Walker (middle class)
Bridlington, East Yorkshire

SIR – Many moons ago I spent a most enjoyable period as a paid slave behind the bar of a market-town pub and became an expert on the ever-evolving class system. There are four types:

1   Old money: those whose superficial appearance offers few clues of significant wealth, are never demanding, always polite and give significant tips, discreetly pushed under the crockery; the most agreeable class.

2   New money: mostly first-generation wealth, invariably loud and brash, they approach the bar offering a drink for everyone, "Oh, and one for yourself, chief"; a get-up-your-nose class.

3   Trash money: usually those connected with the entertainment or media industries earning vast amounts of money for something wholly transient

and forgettable, they treat paid slaves as something nasty stepped in on the pavement; rarely any tips and overwhelmingly the most disagreeable class.

4   No money: always on the scrounge and begging to put things on an already overloaded slate; no tips, obviously, but nevertheless far and away the most entertaining class. Dylan Thomas would be their patron saint.

Huw Beynon
Llandeilo, Carmarthenshire

SIR — A letter you published about classy names sparked fond memories of my service in the Royal Air Force when shortened Christian names became lengthened overnight on the attainment of the rank of Wing Commander: Don to Donald, Pat to Patrick, Bob to Robert, and so on.

Early in my career an ex-public schoolboy called Patrick, then Pat, decreed that I should be known forever as H'Arse, a shortening of my surname. Obviously, I was never destined to achieve great heights as I remain today: Dave H.

Squadron Leader Dave Higginbottom (retd)
Bramhall, Cheshire

HOLDS FORK LIKE SCREWDRIVER

SIR – Why are so many people incapable of using a knife and fork in a conventional manner? Is this because they know no better? Or are they influenced by Hollywood?

At school, over 50 years ago, we were shown the preferred way to hold a knife and fork. You do not use it as a shovel and grasp it as if it were a screwdriver.

I was also taught that when finished, they should be placed neatly side by side on the plate and not just thrown down. However, I suspect that in Ireland older people deliberately place them in the form of a cross.

J.D.K.
Polesworth, Staffordshire

SARTORIAL DYSTOPIA

SIR – There is no television presenter so desperately on trend, no wardrobe malfunction so accidentally forced, no commute so arduous as to justify the sartorial dystopia that is wearing blue jeans with a suit jacket.

Roger Furnell
Welford, Northamptonshire

SIR – Would I be alone in thinking that the British are now the scruffiest and most unkempt people in the world?

Why do young men have to appear unshaven in public at every opportunity? This to me is "unclean".

People of all ages seem to dress abominably on most occasions, and the wearing of a tie would appear to be totally unacceptable.

Dignity in dress has declined, like many aspects of British life, since the arrival of jeans and baseball caps from the United States of America.

Charles James
Bognor Regis, West Sussex

SIR – May I issue a plea to turn the heating down? Now that the colder weather has arrived I cannot walk into an office, shop or railway carriage without instantly producing a mini-Niagara of sweat.

Are people incapable of wearing more than one layer of clothing indoors? Or are they simply looking forward to the day when global warming will mean we can all walk around dressed like *Baywatch* extras?

Bryan R. Shacklady
London EC1

SIR – Since naturists don't have the slightest objection to exposing their unclad bodies, I feel that this makes them ipso facto exhibitionists.

Surely added exposure can only be viewed as free publicity and an attempt to convert the non-believers?

Dr John Gladstone
Gerrards Cross, Buckinghamshire

SIR – I want to know if I am the only person who finds labels itchy and irritating on the neck. The first thing I have to do when buying a new cashmere jumper is to spend 10 minutes trying to unpick the stitching without damaging the knitwear. Strong light and a sharp tool is needed, I can assure you.

I know what the princess on the pea felt like now.

Eva Hancock
Long Itchington, Warwickshire

SIR – Is it just my more sensitive 70-year-old skin, or do others find their Marks & Spencer shirts and underclothes more uncomfortable than in previous years? I am not referring to fit – buying larger sizes accommodates my somewhat enlarged figure – but to the irritation produced by the use of transparent thread to overlock seams. This makes me itch constantly.

I have resorted to wearing my vests inside out,

which brings some relief, but the combination of this thread and a seam down the centre of the back of my boxer shorts makes them unwearable.

Is it just me?

Don Johnson
Chedzoy, Somerset

SIR — Even more annoying than the sound of flip-flops is being behind someone who is a follower of the current trend of wearing their trousers below their buttocks, thereby exposing their pant-clad backsides.

It is not a pretty sight and invariably the wearer has to hitch constantly at their trousers to ensure optimum pant exposure and to avoid full trouser-drop.

The temptation to suggest wearing a belt or braces, or to find a good bit of string, is almost overwhelming at times.

Ginny Hudson
Swanmore, Hampshire

SIR – Yesterday I purchased a new pair of braces. My eyes welled up and a wave of nostalgia flooded over me when I read on the box: "Made in the United Kingdom".

David Laker
Hixon, Staffordshire

SIR – Bill Nighy says that he never trusts a man in linen, but I would never trust a man who wears brown shoes with a grey suit. Who does he think he is: Ken Clarke?

Harry Easu
Charing Heath, Kent

SIR – My mother, born in 1917, told me: "Never trust a man in a bow tie." So far it seems to have been extraordinarily good advice.

Anthony P. Bolton
Aboyne, Aberdeenshire

SIR – What has happened to the good old waterproof codpiece?

J. Burnett-Hewitt
Lowdham, Nottinghamshire

A NATION OF SHOPPERS

SIR – Tonight on the BBC *10 O'clock News* it was reported that a 19-year-old soldier had been killed in Afghanistan.

Seamless segue to the next item: John Lewis report record sales.

Is this what we have become?

David Watkins-Lewis
Bourne End, Buckinghamshire

SIR – Christmas shopping is difficult enough, but am I alone in finding the amplified background "music" tiresome in the extreme?

The constant screeching and wailing often sounds more like souls in torment. It serves only to drive me out of the shop as quickly as possible.

Barry L. Cottle
Harpenden, Hertfordshire

SIR – In the course of a telephone call yesterday I was put on hold and forced to endure almost 10 minutes of the most monotonous music (I use the term loosely) and excruciatingly banal lyrics, including the phrase, "sitting on top of the world in a coin laundry".

Robert Readman
Bournemouth, Dorset

SIR – I am more concerned about my local gym where the pulsating pop music is damaging my hearing in an inverse proportion to my increasing fitness. I have suggested linking the treadmills to the music source so that the harder the customers work, the quieter the music becomes.

As I expected, this has fallen on deaf ears.

Malcolm Allen
Berkhamsted, Hertfordshire

FLAT RANGE CHICKEN

SIR – Whenever I buy a pack of two chicken breasts at my local supermarket, the package contains one large and one small fillet. As an ignorant townie, I wonder if any country-dwelling readers have spotted one of these lop-sided crosses between Audrey Hepburn and Jayne Mansfield (or for the younger generation, Sienna Miller and Kelly Brook) scuttling around in a field?

M.S.
London SE23

SIR – Am I alone in thinking that the quality of KitKats has deteriorated in recent months? My wife and I are finding an increasing number of instances of a wafer inadequately covered in chocolate.

I put it down to quantitative easing.

John Triffitt
Reighton, North Yorkshire

SIR – A recent article reported that confectionery manufacturers were discreetly shrinking the size of their chocolate bars. Is the same thing happening to men's underwear, or am I just getting older?

Michael Cattell
Chester

SIR – Why are there so many pips in lemons these days?

Graham Fearnley
Paddock Wood, Kent

SIR – On being given a banana for the first time, during the Second World War, I ate it with the skin on. I also did this with an orange. Happily, I was later shown the correct way to eat a banana and an orange and grew to like them very much.

George E. Bryant
Bassingham, Lincolnshire

SUPERMARKET SOAP OPERAS

SIR – While in a supermarket recently I suddenly noticed that my poppy had fallen off. Before I could pick it up, a lady retrieved it, affixed it to her coat and strode out.

She was one of the many that "use the lavatory facilities in passing", as it were.

Our standards are slipping.

Brian B. Peirce
London SE3

SIR – I was in the checkout queue in the supermarket today and the woman in front of me was buying an enormous bargain pack of lavatory rolls. As she gave the woman her change the checkout girl said: "Mind how you go."

Nora Jackson
Uttoxeter, Staffordshire

WHO YOU GONNA CALL?

SIR – I keep getting unidentified phone calls at home asking if I'd like to have unlimited calls – but as all the work has gone to China who might there be to call: Ghostbusters?

J.G. Dawson
Chorley, Lancashire

SIR — We are bombarded daily with telephone calls from a far-off land, from people we don't know, asking the shallow question, "How are you today?"

A speedy and efficient way to end such calls is to reply: "Not well at all; my mother has just died."

I can recommend it.

Ian Wilkinson
Homefield, Hertfordshire

SIR — Yesterday evening I received a "cold" telephone call from someone wishing to sell me something. I informed him that I was recording his call for the purpose of training the rest of my family in how to respond to such calls. He terminated the call instantly.

Roy Williams
Aberporth, Ceredigion

MYTH OF THE MALE MENOPAUSE

SIR — I agree wholeheartedly with your report that the male menopause is a myth. For the menopause to occur one must have experienced, and come through, puberty. I know of few such males.

Jennifer Nield
Bristol

SIR – Would it not have been useful if whoever created man had left behind a user's manual?

Peter Boxall
Buckhurst Hill, Essex

SIR – These women must be stopped. First of all we had a 16-year-old girl sailing round the world and now we have a 22-year-old woman climbing Everest. If things go on like this I will have to put down my beer, stop watching television all day and do something.

Graham Senior-Milne
Norham, Northumberland

SIR – There's another word for multi-tasking: incompetence. Just look at the state we're in with all these females: Who do they think they're kidding, apart from themselves and their cohorts of fawning wimps masquerading as males?

David Thomas
Ystradowen, Carmathenshire

SECRETLY LOATHING SANTA

SIR – We still hear regular stories of unacceptable sexual discrimination against women in the office. However, in the run-up to Christmas lots of male office workers have to suffer all sorts of girly activities that they loathe. Do you know any man who actually enjoys Secret Santa? I don't.

Clive Pilley
Westcliff-on-Sea, Essex

G DOESN'T MARK THE SPOT

SIR – As a teenage male I had no end of trouble unsuccessfully attempting to locate this G-spot, which I put down to my dyslexia. Now, you report, it doesn't exist.

This has changed my whole perception of my previous endeavours.

Nigel A. Spry
Hesketh Bank, Lancashire

SIR – No wonder most men cannot find a woman's G-Spot if it is all in the mind. Most men don't understand that a woman has a mind of her own.

Marie J. Jones
Wallington, Surrey

SIR – A current West Sussex NHS advertisement on the back of a bus states: "You are twice as likely to have unprotected sex after heavy drinking".

Another pint, please, landlord.

Robert Price
Haywards Heath, West Sussex

SIR – My first thought on seeing your headline, "Pupils to be taught about sex at seven" was, "What, in the morning?"

When I was a child, the school day began with prayer. But you can't stop progress.

Peter Homer
Highworth, Wiltshire

DOES EVERYONE HATE DADDY?

SIR – About 20 years ago, when we were moving to a new house, I explained to my six-year-old that Daddy, whom she knew was called Richard, would be referred to as Dick by old friends living nearby.

My young daughter went very quiet, and after a few moments, asked in a whispered, concerned voice, "But that doesn't mean that Daddy is a d***head, does it?"

L.L.
Radernie, Fife

SMACK OF FIRM PARENTING

SIR – With the prospect of a ban on smacking one's children on the cards, let us hope that budget airlines manage to weather the recession so that we may, if the situation demands, pack the little darlings on to a cheap flight to a non-EU country and administer the required thrashing with impunity.

I must admit I have borrowed the idea from the CIA and MI6.

Stuart Seear
Newlyn, Cornwall

SIR – With regret I have decided to abandon any attempt to have my autobiography published. I lay the blame for this decision squarely at the door of those who failed to sexually abuse me as a child.

Alan Duncalf
Bampton, Devon

SIR – At last I have a decent excuse to avoid my children's Christmas carol service; I have not been vetted by our Government's child protection team.

Neil Crammond
Limpsfield, Surrey

SIR — We are experiencing dark times but my children have a solution to lighten our burden. I thought they were studying hard for their forthcoming examinations, but it seems that they are actually obsessed with a new craze which involves changing the word "wand" to "willy" in Harry Potter quotes.

A couple of examples:

— "There have been stories about an unbeatable willy for years," said Hermione.

— "My willy!" said Ron, in a shaky voice. "Look at my willy!" It had snapped, almost in two; the tip was dangling limply, held on by a few splinters.

Philip Armstrong
Bodle Street Green, East Sussex

SIR — As a youngster growing up in the war, I had no problems with boredom. I had a ball. In the winter I kicked it; in the summer I bowled it. It kept me out of trouble for hours on end.

John C. Simmons
Silkstone, South Yorkshire

SIR – I was delighted to see my eldest son and his wife over Christmas, but was somewhat surprised to see that he wears a flat cap while driving a Volvo estate.

At what age is it normal for a man to be seen so attired? He is only 30.

Thomas Bowler
Little Houghton, Northamptonshire

WHEN I'M 106

SIR – When discussing the pros and cons of old age with my clergyman grandfather just after his 102nd birthday he commented: "When you get to 100, dear boy, you will find that if you drink more than a bottle of claret a day, your legs will go wobbly."

He ignored his own advice at his 106th birthday party, fell and died of the complications three months later.

There is clearly a careful balance to be struck here.

Philip M.M. Collings
Dorchester on Thames, Oxfordshire

SIR – Having reached that certain age, I have been the recipient of a test kit from the NHS Bowel Cancer Screening Programme. While I consider this to be a tremendous initiative in assisting in the early detection of cancer, how do I answer my grandchildren when they ask, "Did you enjoy Pooh-sticks, Grandad?"?

> **P.E.**
> Tilehurst, Berkshire

SIR – Despite being 70 I still often cover the back of my envelopes with "Burma" (Be undressed ready, my Angel) and "Norwich" (Knickers off ready when I come home), albeit without much response.

> **Dick Kemp**
> Greenhithe, Kent

SIR – Last week my wife and I (combined age 141) carried a double oven from the car boot into the house. It probably weighed a couple of hundredweight. We then carried the old one out and took it to the tip.

If my school arithmetic is still serviceable, that's about double the weight that a Calor executive claims his workers can't manage between them.

Oh, and we're still standing.

> **Colin Standing**
> Kendal, Cumbria

SIR — I read your article on a local council giving older people advice on the safe fitting of slippers with great interest. As a 67-year-old motorcyclist I am wondering if my local council might offer me advice on how to put my boots on safely — at taxpayers' expense, naturally.

Martin Hands
Ilkeston, Derbyshire

SIR — Today I received my English Heritage Membership card. On the front is printed: "Dr J.P. Lester — Expires end of June 2011."
  How can they possibly know?

John Lester
Walsall, West Midlands

SIR — Martin Amis calls for "euthanasia booths" where elderly people can end their lives with "a Martini and a medal".
  I will gladly buy him a double if he is the first into the booth.

Gerard Parke-Hatton
Broughton, Lancashire

SIR — I am close to my sell-by date and am endowed with the experience, prejudices and perceptions this gives. However, I am sufficiently open-minded to realise that our country's future lies in the hands of a younger and more imaginative generation.

If the grandees and war horses of all political colours are unable to accept this and support the new order, please will they steal away to some distant meadow and chunter quietly among themselves.

Colin Cummings
Yelvertoft, Northamptonshire

SIR — Discussing how we had aged over the past 10 years, my husband and I agreed that the main sign is that we now hold hands to cross the road.

J. Campanini Russell
Twickenham, Middlesex

SPORTING TRIUMPH AND DISASTER

BUGGER THE OLYMPICS

SIR – Imagine my horror last week when I was offered 10 freshly minted Olympic stamps – more than two years before the big event.

I asked: "Have you any that say 'Bugger the Olympics'?" To my delight, this drew smiles and a wry cheer from my fellow customers.

It was good to learn that I am not alone.

David Armstrong
Hipperholme, West Yorkshire

SIR – The people in charge of coming up with your Olympic mascots missed a terrific opportunity to show what the British people truly bring to the world.

You should have had a greasy, pasty, overweight lout with rotten black teeth and bad body odour. He could have been holding a greasy banger in one hand and chips in the other.

Then we would see the real Britain, in all its glory.

J.C.
Ontario, Canada

SIR – Far from spending less money on the opening ceremony of the 2012 Olympic Games, I would prefer more to be spent. The opening ceremony is the only part of the games I enjoy.

Wendy Rowlands
Cotheridge, Worcestershire

TIGER'S BIRDIES

SIR – Having seen pictures of some of Tiger Woods's acquaintances, I'm thinking of taking up golf.

Geoff Hall
Worcester Park, Surrey

SIR – Rather than pursuing ladies, Tiger Woods might try taking up a hobby. May I suggest golf?

Nicholas Chittenden
Herodsfoot, Cornwall

SIR – I think Tiger Woods should apologise to the women with whom he didn't have affairs. There can't be many and they must feel very lonely and neglected.

Anne M. Brown
Bingley, West Yorkshire

SIR – Golf enthusiasts around the world are no doubt beside themselves with frustration at the inadequacy of reporting on Tiger Woods's car accident. They are informed that Mrs Woods rescued her husband by smashing the car's rear window with a golf club. But which club did she use?

John Riseley
Harrogate, North Yorkshire

SIR – The only surprise for me about the Tiger Woods saga is that a man of his wealth would drive a Cadillac Escalade.

Sqn Ldr Gerry Walsh RAF (retd)
Greylees, Lincolnshire

CAPTAIN CHAV

SIR – I'm not sure whether John Terry is being pilloried for infidelity to his wife or to an ex team-mate. Either way, it seems to me he was the perfect choice to captain the rest of the chavs who represent the country.

Chris Jeffs
Borehamwood, Hertfordshire

SIR – After reading the ongoing debate as to whether John Terry has lost the captain's armband, I feel he need only check under Wayne Bridge's bed.

J.C.
Bexhill-On-Sea, East Sussex

SIR – It is clear to me that John Terry's haircut alone should be enough to relieve him of the responsibility of captaincy.

Patrick Ryecart
London SW10

SIR – I heard a journalist suggesting that the national sport of Britain was under threat. Au contraire, the prurient sniggering suggests that the national sport of Britain is in the rudest of health.

Mike Cooper
Market Harborough, Leicestershire

SIR – Just before the furore dies down, does anyone actually know what a football captain does?

Bob Lovett
Earls Colne, Essex

SIR – Who else remembers when professional footballers were paid £10 per week?

Stan Procter
Tadworth, Surrey

WATCHING THE WINTER OLYMPICS

SIR – Let's be honest: how many of us are watching the Winter Olympics for the crashes? Perhaps less so after the fatality, but let's not be hypocrites about this.

Phil Bailey
Crickhowell, Powys

SIR – I am seriously disappointed that there isn't a Freestyle Road Gritting Competition in the Winter Olympics.

Peter Ellis
Ripon, North Yorkshire

SIR – Some say that rowing facing backwards is mildly ridiculous, but a grown-up person sitting on a piece of metal and careering feet-first down a tunnel of ice at 85mph is quite absurd.

Richard Evans
Evercreech, Somerset

PRETTY IN ALL BLACK

SIR – The invasion of female commentators on rugby union is unacceptable. It is hard to listen to some silly girl concentrate on the attractiveness of a shirt's colour rather than the thuggery that is taking place before her.

Lt Col Dale Hemming-Tayler (retd)
Driffield, Gloucestershire

SIR – I have said this before, but I say it again: the BBC has got to stop its PC assault on the game of rugby by using so many ignorant female commentators. Listening to Gabby Logan talk about fashion and cold hands in the warm-up period to the France v Ireland game was the final straw. We talk beef, not salad dressing.

Lt Col Dale Hemming-Tayler (retd)
Driffield, Gloucestershire

SIR – Could you sometimes leave a picture of Martin Johnson out of your sport supplement? We all know by now what he looks like – poor fellow – and you are frightening the horses.

J.G.
Walton on the Naze, Essex

SIR – My enjoyment of the France v Ireland match on Saturday was ruined by the insistence of Eddie Butler on pronouncing the names of the French players in the most ridiculous Inspector Clouseau accent. As he does not adopt a Taggart brogue when commentating on matches involving Scotland, or a Bertie Wooster tone for England's, can anyone explain this absurd affectation?

Alison Cotton
Shrewton, Wiltshire

SIR – I read that Jonny Wilkinson is advising rugby players to drink one and a half litres of Volvic mineral water a day to keep them "hydrated, active and alert". What's wrong with strong lager?

Roger Marsh
Morecambe, Lancashire

DOUGHTY WILLOW-WIELDERS

SIR – Will someone please tell television and radio commentators that those doughty men who wield the willow are "batsmen" not "batters". They make them sound like labourers in fish and chip shops.

Ian Thomas
Aspley Guise, Buckinghamshire

SIR – I was so distressed to hear that the honour of leading his country has jaded Andrew Strauss, and that he has asked for a rest. Poor thing!

Mr Strauss should, in my opinion, be stripped of the captaincy forever following this appallingly spineless outburst.

Where have all of the real leaders of men gone, for God's sake?

Ian Mackenzie
Barnoldby le Beck, Lincolnshire

SIR – If David Cameron wishes to secure his place in English history all he needs to do is bring back cricket to Freeview TV and ensure that it stays there.

William Denis Browne
Bridport, Dorset

SIR – Some believe in fairies, others that the world is flat. But, most astonishingly of all, a few still rate Kevin Pietersen.

Clive Lawrence
Gillingham, Kent

CHERIE MURRAY

SIR – So Andy Murray has not made his mind up whether he will bow to the Queen at Wimbledon. Perhaps he should change his name to Cherie Murray – we all know how unpopular she is.

Barbara Stead
Newbury, Berkshire

SIR – Am I alone in wishing Andy Murray would either shave or grow a proper beard? His scruffy appearance does nothing to enhance his standing as a sporting ambassador of this country.

Michael O'Connor
Hertford

SIR – I am concerned for the hygiene of the splendid ranks of ball boys and girls. Being constantly handed towels that have been the subject of facial ablutions by sweaty players is surely wrong. Maybe flesh-coloured, disposable rubber gloves could be provided?

Jon Carter
Great Yarmouth, Norfolk

SIR — Let us hope that, as Andy Murray matures as a tennis player, he will drop the habit of giving Great Ape impressions when he wins. They are uncannily accurate, but aurally and visually unpleasant. They also detract greatly from his dignity as a sportsman, and lower the standing of his sport. Has nobody told him?

R. Dixon
Mansfield, Nottinghamshire

SIR — Sadly, after two fairytale weeks, Andy Murray becomes Scottish again.

Simon Sinclair
Romiley, Cheshire

WORLD CUP REFUSENIKS

SIR — Please, to save my sanity, would someone, somewhere, invent a device that plays anything — a recording of cats yowling would do — every time the words "World Cup", "football" or "England" are broadcast on the radio?

Brenda Frisby
Cottesmore, Leicestershire

SIR – Whose idea was it to stage the World Cup during the cricket season?

Mary E. Rudd
Pevensey Bay, East Sussex

SIR – I am so pleased World Cup football is with us again. It's much easier to spot a vehicle flying a flag than one being driven by an individual wearing a baseball cap or a hoodie.

Andrew MacDonald
Lutton, Lincolnshire

SIR – Can we appeal for help to continue our research into the size of appendages among British men: could all those with extremely small members make themselves known over the next three weeks by flying a white flag with a red cross on their cars?

D.L.
Edgcumbe, Cornwall

SIR – When I was an 11-year-old schoolboy, I was pilloried in front of the class by a waspish schoolmarm because I admitted a lack of interest in football. Seventy-two years later I still cannot see the merit in watching 22 overpaid thickheads kicking, cuddling and posturing on muddy turf.

When a goal is scored, why does the player run around, arms akimbo, gob agape, behaving like a spoilt brat, as though to say, "Look at me, mummy! Aren't I a clever little boy?"

After which the other players all go into a group cuddle like a bunch of teenage schoolgirls celebrating their A-level results.

And, if we must suffer television interviews, could the players not be coached in basic elocution and English grammar?

Yours in despair,
Harry Smith
Welwyn Garden City, Hertfordshire

SIR – How patriotic it makes me feel to see all these England flags fluttering from the windows of BMWs, Mercedes, Audis, Nissans, Toyotas, etc.

Stuart Smith
Houghton, Cambridgeshire

SIR – I am no lover of football and have not seen any matches played in the World Cup. However, on the news I have seen clips of the pre-match national anthems, and I have yet to see Wayne Rooney open his mouth in time to the music.

Has the boy got no respect for Queen and country? Perhaps if the millions of patriotic royalists were to line up in front of Rooney and take it in turns to give him a slap by way of reminder, he might, after the first few million slaps, get it into his thick head.

Paul Morley
Romford, Essex

SIR – Why is it that the only sportsmen who spit regularly are soccer players?

Michael Patterson
Burgundy, France

SIR – Is it all over now? Did we win?

Felicity Foulis Brown
Bramley, Hampshire

THE VUVUZELA'S COMING HOME...

SIR — If you think the background drone of vuvuzelas at the World Cup is irritating, just wait until the fans return to England, every one of them convinced that he is the only one to think of the brilliant wheeze of toting home one of these instruments to enliven Saturday nights on the town.

They will be a novel addition to the traditional squealing, bawling, fighting and leaving displays of rainbow vomit every few yards along the pavement — which, for the benefit of puzzled foreigners, is called "having a good time".

Peter Wyton
Longlevens, Gloucestershire

SIR — I have found that a long cardboard tube makes a very good vuvuzela. I've not yet managed 127 decibels but I have played it loud enough to annoy the family and the dogs.

Nicholas C. Jenkins
Claybrooke Parva, Leicestershire

SIR – I was delighted to hear two young girls in Ringwood town centre last Saturday serenading the shoppers with their vuvuzelas.

They managed to drown out the boom-boom emanating from the blacked-out hatchbacks.

Sally Withers
Ringwood, Hampshire

SIR – I, too, am becoming increasingly disgruntled by the incessant buzz of vuvuzelas. Could I suggest that they be banned and replaced by the quaint and reassuringly familiar English ditty: "You're gonna get your f****** head kicked in."

C.H.
Kent

...BUT THE WORLD CUP ISN'T

SIR – All that hype about the England team "lifting the World Cup". They couldn't even lift a fairy cake.

Kelvin Shuffell
Tisbury, Wiltshire

SIR – Did I see Emile Heskey state that he's a striker? Presumably this means he has joined a union which has called him out on strike, along with all his team mates.

Hubert Allen
Welham Green, Hertfordshire

SIR – I thought English footballers like John Terry and Ashley Cole were good at playing away from home. What went wrong?

John Reynolds
Huntingdon, Cambridgeshire

SIR – I think that I have found the cause of the England football team's woeful performance: tattoos. The majority of the players are adorned with some form of body art.

Compare this with the finalists, Spain and Holland, who seem to have comparatively ink-free skin.

Perhaps in future the England team should be selected on this basis, and not on their perceived ability.

Robert Taylor
Bury St Edmunds, Suffolk

SIR – Watching uninspiring football is bad enough but constantly seeing "I'm lovin' it" on the screen merely rubs salt into the wound.

Robert Fromow
London SW1

SIR – I have learnt one thing from England's defeat: there are 11 other Englishmen and one Italian who know even less about World Cup football than I do, which in my case, amounts to diddly squat.

Brian Smith
Weston-Super-Mare, Somerset

SIR – I offer myself as the next England manager. I am reasonably good-looking, I speak good English, and I do not follow the Italian method of advancing backwards.

John Wallis
Hartford, Cambridgeshire

SIR – I trust that on their return the England team will make the usual tour of central London in an open-top bus, so that fans can show their appreciation.

Don Roberts
Wirral

HOME
THOUGHTS
ON ABROAD

IDF V MY CCF

SIR – Am I the only person to be absolutely stunned by the fact that a fully armed crack commando unit of the legendary Israeli Defence Force was overwhelmed on a planned military raid by a group of civilians, both male and female, who set about the unfortunate soldiers with chairs, clubs and knives, threw the odd commando overboard, and then disarmed two of them and used the weapons to fire at the raiding party?

Will the IDF ever get over this or are they destined to become the laughing stock of commando units everywhere?

My old school's CCF could have done a far better job than this fiasco.

Saker Nusseibeh
London SW7

BP AND BABY BARACK

SIR – President Obama's behaviour towards BP resembles that of a spoiled, overindulged child. It's long overdue that he heard the words, "No, you can't."

Lawrence Fraser
Elgin, Moray

SIR – If Barack Obama continues to call BP by its former name, maybe we should consider returning the favour and calling him by his initials.

Paul Anders
Chorleywood, Hertfordshire

SIR – Perhaps BP should revert to its even older name: Anglo-Iranian Oil Company. Or would that pour oil on troubled waters?

M.P.
Hove, East Sussex

SIR – If reports are to be believed, President Obama has one boot on the throat of British pensioners while "kicking ass" – presumably Tony Hayward's – with the other. A singular feat indeed, even for an American, given that he and the pensioners are on opposite sides of the Atlantic.

Richard Shaw
Dunstable, Bedfordshire

SIR – Ever since I heard that the BP Chairman, Carl-Henric Svanberg, has been summoned to meet President Obama, I've had this silly ditty going round in my head to the tune of "Oh Susanna". With apologies:

I'm off to see Obama 'cos I'm chairman of BP,
He's gonna kick my ass for pouring oil into the sea.
There's fifty thousand barrels escaping every day,
But I'll just take my lickin' and then I'll be on my way

Chorus:

Oh, Obama, you don't frighten me.
We'll keep right on a'drilling in that little ole North Sea.

Allan Britton
Cwmbran, Gwent

SIR – Obama's revenge: BP oil on Robert Green's goalkeeping gloves.

H.H.
Manchester

SIR – Barack Obama has given up smoking. That explains everything.

Brian Ager
Roydon, Norfolk

HORSE-WHIPPING BERLUSCONI

SIR – *Pace* the man who attacked Silvio Berlusconi and broke his nose, study of Alan Clark's career surely suggests that the most appropriate instrument with which to belabour a serial philanderer is a horsewhip.

Professor Martyn Rady
Ramsgate, Kent

SIR – I am intrigued that anyone who attacks a public figure is described as a "mental patient". In the case of Mr Berlusconi, I would have thought the desire to attack demonstrated sanity.

Russ King
London N11

SIR – Am I the only one surprised that Mr Berlusconi has not already been punched on the nose after being confronted by an irate husband or father?

Ted Shorter
Hildenborough, Kent

SIR — Silvio Berlusconi and Nicolas Sarkozy are both apparently at it. Come on, Gordon Brown. Do you want to be a leading European politician or not?

Michael Knight
Swadlincote, Derbyshire

SIR — I well remember the time when a French gynaecologist was the guest speaker at an education day I attended. He said that his research had shown that around 15 to 20 per cent of husbands were impotent for a time after watching their wives giving birth.

In a truly splendid French touch he added: "This, fortunately, is only as far as their wives are concerned."

C.C.
Canada

DIM VIEW OF THE EU

SIR — Every evening when I switch on my dim, twisted, EU-approved light bulbs I am reminded of my resolve not to vote for the dim and twisted politicians who treacherously denied us the opportunity to vote on membership of the community.

P.R. Pendleton
Westerham, Kent

SIR – We don't want a centrally controlled EU.
We want our bent carrots and warm beer sold by the
pint, and sweets sold in ounces. We don't want
foreigners with unpronounceable names who can't
say "th" telling us what to do. We don't want a
referendum on the Lisbon Treaty in order to
canvass public opinion; we want it so we can vote
"no" and give all those garlic-eaters a jolly good
two-fingered salute.

If we have to answer to corrupt politicians, we
want to answer to our own, home-grown corrupt
politicians.

Anthony D.M. Peters
Great Rollright, Oxfordshire

SIR – It seems to me that while Britain remains in
the EU, the only bit of our sovereignty we are likely
to retain is our sovereign debt.

Mike Bridgeman
Market Lavington, Wiltshire

SIR – I have a Swiss friend to whom I once
mentioned that Switzerland had not joined the EU.

"Ah no," she said. "We may be small, but we are
not stupid."

How true! How true!

Patrick J. Ellis
Eggesford, Devon

SIR – The Germans MAKE the law.
The French READ the law.
The British OBEY the law.
Why are we so pathetic?
Could we not be like the French sometimes
and REVOLT?

Mrs D.L.

STORM IN A VATICAN TEACUP

SIR – What a relief to hear Benedict XVI dismiss
coverage of the child sex scandals, currently
destroying the Catholic Church, as "petty gossip".

Perhaps His Holiness can now turn his attention
to the storm in a teacup which was Papal silence
during the Holocaust?

Anthony Lord
Thornton-Cleveleys, Lancashire

SIR – Did the Roman Catholic Church take the
words, "Suffer the little children" the wrong way?

S.C.
Hougham, Lincolnshire

SIR – If, as I believe, there is a connection between celibacy and the sexual abuse of children by some Catholic priests, why doesn't the Church introduce castration into the rites of passage for priesthood? After all, they will have no further use for their tackle.

Rodney de Cani
Tarvin, Cheshire

SIR – The press is reporting that the current scandal in the Catholic Church has become a witch hunt against the Pope. If so, then the same rules the Church used to advocate against witches should be applied: throw the Pope in the nearest river. If he sinks, he's innocent; if he floats, he's guilty and should be burnt at the stake.

Alternatively, to compensate victims around the world, the cardinals could sell some of their bling and expensive dresses.

I have no doubt Jesus would have agreed with the latter option.

Phil Bailey
Crickhowell, Powys

MAHMOUD DINNER JACKET

SIR – Holidaying with a number of other teenagers in North Wales before the Second World War we found it almost impossible to pronounce any of the names which confronted us on the map. We therefore devised our own English equivalents; the only one I can remember now is "land on your stomach".

As this device is applicable to any language or place, the President of Iran will always be Mr Dinner Jacket to me.

James Sayers
Avening, Gloucestershire

DUBAI ASSASSINATION PANTOMIME

SIR – Now that there are no fewer than 26 suspects for the assassination in Dubai, it is more likely that this pathetically inept pantomime was enacted not by Mossad, but by the British Home Office.

Just how many people do you need to eradicate an unaccompanied arms dealer?

Tony Jones
Eastbury, Berkshire

SIR – I am shocked, utterly shocked, by the suggestion that an assassination team would use faked passports.

Kenneth Hynes
London N7

AFGHAN SONGS OF PRAISE

SIR – I have just heard on Radio 4 a brief clip of troops in Afghanistan rehearsing for the Armistice Day service. I have never heard such a dreary, dismal drag in my life. "Amazing Grace" sounded more like "Dissolving Grease".

They must have some leisure time. I don't know how they spend it, but surely some organised social activity such as a choir would help to relieve the tension?

If a couple of hundred POWs in the Second World War could inspire the likes of Benjamin Britten to write a major male-voice work for them, out of our 14,000 or so troops in Afghanistan the right person – such as the wonderful Gareth Malone from the BBC series, *The Choir* – could produce a most impressive choir.

It might even suggest to the locals that we Westerners have a little bit of culture.

Geoffrey Shaw
Sanderstead, Surrey

NAOMI CAMPBELL'S BULLET-PROOF DRESS

SIR – I try to imagine myself as a young, beautiful, rich model staying alone in a hotel room in a relatively volatile country. The time is very late in the evening, I am already asleep in bed, and suddenly there is a knock on the door. What would be my instinctive reaction?

A   Summon urgent help from hotel security.
B   Put on a bullet-proof dress, hold my trusted Colt/Walther PPK ready in my hand and, standing to the side of the door, ask for the ID of the unexpected caller to be slipped under the door.
C   Just open the door to see who it was.

Elli Ron
Fetcham, Surrey

SIR – Why is Naomi Campbell called a "super" model? She is not even a good role model.

Jeremy Nicholas
Great Bardfield, Essex

SIR – I thought that a supermodel opening her bedroom door in the middle of the night to two unexpected men was a schoolboy fantasy.

Philip Howells
Walkden, Lancashire

OU EST LA PLUME DE TA TANTE?

SIR – I am continually amazed at how foreign languages are taught in British schools. Having lived in France for the past 13 years, I have yet to have anyone ask me the whereabouts of "la plume de ma tante" or "le bureau de mon oncle" – both phrases that were battered into my consciousness during French lessons at school.

P. B-S
Badefols sur Dordogne, France

SIR – I always understood that the three essential phrases for the gentleman traveller were: "Lie down, I wish to speak with you"; "Take off your clothes, I cannot hear"; and "My friend will pay".

Roger Welby-Everard
Caythorpe, Nottinghamshire

SIR – On the last working day before Christmas, my office organised a "Secret Santa" ceremony. As a result, I received an item of confectionery moulded to resemble a certain portion of the female anatomy. The manufacturer of said item clearly had an eye to the export trade, as the ingredients label was multi-lingual. As a result, I can now say "chocolate boobies" in six European languages.

S.H.
Brentwood, Essex

THE WIRELESS
AND THE
GOGGLEBOX

RADIO GAGA

SIR — I swear that if I hear *Ride of the Valkyries* again on Classic FM, I may not be responsible for my actions.

David Watt
Thame, Oxfordshire

SIR — I worry about the way John Humphrys bullies our leaders on the *Today* programme. I worry also about myself as I enjoy listening and frequently find myself cheering as they squirm under his lash. Does this mean I am a sadist?

Gordon Garment
Chipping, Lancashire

SIR — What on earth is going on at Radio 2 at the moment? We've got Graham Norton sitting in for Chris Evans in the morning, and Dale Winton covering Steve Wright in the afternoon. It's as camp as a row of tents.

Throw in Alan Carr for Ken Bruce next week and we'll have a full-on jamboree.

Steve Brennan
Glenmavis, Lanarkshire

IN THE CHAIR WITH CHRIS EVANS

SIR – While sitting in the waiting room at my dentist I could not help but hear the sound of Chris Evans on Radio 2, which I have so far managed to avoid. It was far worse than I had feared. He has no talent whatsoever.

It was a relief to be called into the dentist's surgery. The possibility of root canal treatment is a far less worrying prospect than having to listen to Evans's high-pitched voice again.

John Thomas
Great Boughton, Cheshire

SIR – Alas for the decent and seemly generation. Wogan and his like are now all gone. The world has undoubtedly changed. Chris Evans's avowals and promises are worthless. Our generation must accept a modified version of L.P. Hartley's famous remark. We must now say: "The present is a foreign country. They do things differently here."

C.J.G. Macy
Wellingore, Lincolnshire

SIR – Has anyone heard Chris Evans play a song from beginning to end without interrupting with his inane prattling? I am trying to like the man, but, well....

Norman Scott
Stacklawhill, Ayrshire

SIR – Woebegone! From bright wit to dim wit. Evans sent – somewhere quiet, please.

Kenneth Vickers
Blackpool

SIR – BBC Radio Norfolk. Peace reigns again.

R.G.
Norwich

SIR – Listening to the smooth voice of Ken Clarke on Radio 4 has made me wish for the BBC to realise what a mistake they've made.

Marguerite Beard-Gould
Walmer, Kent

SIR – I believe Jimmy Young is still available.

Stephen Smith
Wokingham, Berkshire

GOOD WIDDANCE TO WOSSY

SIR – I understand from my showbiz friends, of whom I have none, that Jonathan Ross is leaving the BBC.

Hurrah and huzzah!

Jeff Howe
Eastry, Kent

SIR – I read that Jonathan Ross "can't wait" to leave the BBC. I had thought it impossible to be in complete agreement with him but I can't wait either.

Martin Freye
Stoke Bishop, Somerset

SIR – What a self-indulgent little twerp Jonathan Ross is, thinking that he is disliked only by "a handful of idiots who write for a Right-wing newspaper".

Political persuasion has nothing to do with it: I am not "Right wing" and I think his output is nothing but distasteful garbage.

Richard Hartley
Mistley, Essex

SIR — Who is Jonathan Ross?

Bharat Jashanmal
Fairford, Gloucestershire

SIR — Let us hope he finds new employment, very
soon — preferably in China or North Korea.

John F.M. Rodwell
London W8

FIONA BRUCE'S BUM ATTIRE

SIR — Am I alone in noticing the contrast between
the attire of Fiona Bruce presenting *Victoria: a Royal
Love Story* and David Dimbleby's appearance as the
dapper, quintessential Englishman presenting *Seven
Ages of Britain*?

As Miss Bruce toured our wonderful royal palaces
the camera focused frequently on a rear view of her
short jacket over skin-tight denims. In the section
on Balmoral the eye was drawn from the magnificent
Highland scenery to Miss Bruce's dazzling, scarlet
PVC jacket.

Could not Miss Bruce redirect some of her
£500,000 salary to the hiring of a wardrobe
consultant? Surely she could afford some elegant
British fashions in natural tweed and linen?

U.B.
Cowes, Isle of Wight

SIR – Has David Dimbleby made a bulk purchase of pink shirts for *Seven Ages of Britain*?

Jennie Graham
Colchester, Essex

SIR – Am I alone in thinking what a scruffy appearance a lot of men present on television by wearing open-necked shirts with a jacket? Why don't they just discard the jacket and be completely improperly dressed?

L.E.
London SE6

SIR – Sian Williams says she enjoys her job so much that she would appear in the buff on breakfast television. I am looking forward to it; it would be an improvement on some of the clothes she wears.

Leslie Watson
Swansea

ROLLING NEWSREADERS

SIR – In pressing the BBC for older women to read the news, Harriet Harman makes the classic mistake of forgetting the views of the customer. Newsreaders, whether male or female, should not take on the job unless they are prepared to accept early and graceful retirement. We would not expect the England cricket team to field Sir Ian Botham.

Geoffrey Evans
Digswell, Hertfordshire

SIR – Old codgers like me are happier to see an attractive newsreader, which usually means a younger one.

Perhaps Harriet Harman's crusade for equality should press the BBC to have Scottish, Irish and Welsh newsreaders for their regional news, and allow us English to have English newsreaders; we would then have a chance of understanding what they're saying.

John Nicholl
Royston, Hertfordshire

SIR — I am aggravated beyond tolerance by the
fodder of botoxed flesh, flashing gnashers,
dead-mice-on-heads, anorexic bodies with pendants
pointing the way down cleavages — and, worst of all,
the twee, downturned, pseudo-serious mouth.

Sometimes we get a change of newsreader.
Sometimes I flick to the other channel. And what do
I find? Clones.

Jean M. Shackleton
Norwich

SIR — I am extremely irritated by the constant
gesturing of television reporters. They can "tear a
passion" over the most mundane event. The worst
look like demented windmills.

J.R. Firth
Edwinstowe, Nottinghamshire

SCORING THE WEATHER FORECAST

SIR – Isn't it time we started classifying the track record of weather forecasters?

Like the matrix in diving competitions for the degree of difficulty, there would have to be factors that credited accurate long-range forecasting and reduced the score for more predictable areas or times of the year.

It is surely time we knew whether a piece of seaweed or a finger in the air would give as good a prediction as the questionable professional skills of meteorologists.

Michael Archer
London SW20

SIR – Am I alone in thinking that the Met Office forecasts were somewhat more reliable when the organisation was billeted on the Air Ministry Roof?

David Dixon
Hastings, Sussex

SIR – As the snow is now less likely to hit the southeast as hard, I hear the Met Office has changed the status of its weather warning from "Severe" to "Couldn't Give a Toss".

Phil Bailey
Crickhowell, Powys

SIR – Why do female weather forecasters dress as if they have just dropped in from a party?

Ann Jeater
Wokingham, Berkshire

TELEVISION DEMOCRACY

SIR – Last night I was waiting for a film to start and found myself watching the last 15 minutes of *Celebrity Big Brother*. Is this really what people want? If so, I see no future for the human race. Incidentally, I did not recognise any of the "celebrities".

Peter Walton
Buckingham

SIR — I couldn't vote for the EU. I couldn't vote for the Lisbon Treaty. But I can vote for *Strictly Come Dancing*. Hooray!

S.H.
Cossington, Somerset

SIR — Having, under duress, watched the latest edition of *Britain's Got Talent*, I'm wondering if the show's producers might have a case to answer under the Trade Descriptions Act.

Pitiful, and cruel.

Andrea Hunt
Datchet, Berkshire

THE X-RATED FACTOR

SIR — Our Government is keen to put warning labels on everything from food to electrical goods. So why not television programmes? They could be rated according to the intelligence required from the viewer.

So the *X Factor* could have a "Really dumb" rating; BBC News a "Below-average intelligence" score; Channel Four News an "Above-average intelligence" warning; and *Mastermind* and *University Challenge* a "Working brain essential" label.

This would enable people in today's dumbed-down Britain to choose programmes that would not overtax their capabilities, thereby possibly damaging their self-esteem and mental health.

David Craig
Bournemouth, Dorset

SIR – I would like to place on record that I have never watched the *X Factor*, and do not intend to do so in future. What has happened to this country that we have become so obsessed with those who lack talent?

Reggie Byram
Elland, West Yorkshire

SIR – Can someone explain the *X Factor* to me? I do not have a television set.

Eddie Peart
Rotherham, South Yorkshire

SIR – Will the second coming take place on the *X Factor*?

Alan Field
Scarrington, Nottinghamshire

BOTTOM GEAR

SIR – Watching Jeremy Clarkson and his band of *Top Gear* heroes drive around a sugar cane plantation pretending to battle bamboo in the heart of the South American rainforest pretty well summed up the year, the decade, and the BBC – expensive and dishonest.

Rex Barron
Ledbury, Herefordshire

SIR – Does a large proportion of our population really find watching very elderly schoolchildren act out their fantasies and do silly things on *Top Gear* edifying? Worst of all are the schoolyard arguments about "cool" or "uncool" cars.

Entertainment? I think not.

Paul Barnes
Garstang, Lancashire

SIR – I was thrilled to see a large picture of James May on the front page of the motoring section with sticky tape across his mouth. I do hope this will be a permanent fixture; he could then give up disturbing the public and play with his toys all day long instead.

I am not being totally unpleasant, as he is better than the other two, but the choice is not great.

Keith Phillips
Milford on Sea, Hampshire

THE BRAIN-WASHING BROADCASTING CORPORATION

SIR – I am beginning to be suspicious about loud music on television documentaries. The BBC, in particular, is well aware that everyone hates it; it has been told often enough.

There must be something sinister behind it. Could it be yet another brain-washing exercise?

Win Clavering
Colsterworth, Lincolnshire

COCKNEY COPPER COCK-UP

SIR – At the conclusion of *EastEnders'* 25th anniversary live episode was I alone in noting that a police officer chased Bradley Branning across the rooftops without having carried out a full risk assessment?

Sqn Ldr Gerry Walsh RAF (retd)
Greylees, Lincolnshire

CRIME AND
PUNISHMENT

MY SON IS SCUM

SIR – "Magistrate who called vandals 'scum' is censured", you report.

That this should happen to a magistrate voicing the thoughts of all right-minded people is absurd – as is the fact that the mother of one of the culprits is to lodge a complaint. No doubt she is looking for thousands in compensation for the little darling's hurt feelings.

Ideally they should all have been put in the stocks and pelted with rotten fruit. Harsh? I think not – in some middle-eastern countries it would be stones.

As for the mother, she should be made to write out 100 times: "My son is scum". The penny may then drop.

Over to you, Theresa May. Middle England awaits redemption.

Malcolm Sweeney
Stockton on Tees

SIR – In 1954 I had to write 200 times the following lines: "I, Michael Leslie Davies, must not indulge in the filthy American habit of masticating gum during the historical studies of my fellow pupils of Form 4b."

Since then I have never chewed gum.

Michael Davies
Pontypool, Gwent

SIR — The "broken society" is easily explained: lack of discipline. Some months before the Second World War, when I was nine years old, I told my father that I was being bullied.

He told me to go to the leader's house, knock on the door and politely ask for the boy. When the lad appeared I was to say "leave me alone" and punch him as hard as possible on the nose, before walking away without another word.

I did; he fell down a bloody mess and all bullying ceased.

Today? Pathetic.

Peter Vivian
Camberley, Surrey

SIR — When I was a boy I behaved well, most of the time, because there was an ingrained disincentive to behave badly. It consisted of public shame, loss of freedom and, quite often, a certain degree of pain — none of which, I emphasise, did me any lasting harm.

Assemble an empowered committee of people of my age, tell Brussels where to shove its Human Rights Act and we will set about restoring the Queen's Peace.

R.M. Stephens
Abingdon, Oxfordshire

SIR — Walking through a local park earlier this week, I heard a mother shouting to her small daughter: "Harmony! Harmony! If she hits you, hit her back."

Naomi Thornton
London SE4

SIR — David Cameron says that we will have more police on our streets. How are we, the public, expected to recognise them after such a long absence?

David Le Clercq
Bournemouth

SIR — Today, in my gentle suburb, I went out taking photographs of houses, trees and people in the snow. Unfortunately, in doing so, I took a photo of a "Community Support Officer", a young woman about five-foot tall dressed in a paramilitary uniform. She immediately came over and demanded that I delete the photo on "security grounds".

Which moron is in charge of this bunch of toy soldiers?

Phil Johnston
Heaton Moor, Lancashire

THE FORWARD OFFENSIVE

SIR – If Munir Hussain had not had a cricket bat to hand he would probably not have committed such a grievous assault on an intruder. Surely this lends weight to the growing feeling that they have no place in a modern, progressive and egalitarian society, and are in fact symbols of a bygone age of elitism and violent oppression.

Cricket bats should be banned.

Richard J. Lawton
Austrey, Warwickshire

SIR – I have no idea how hard or where to hit an intruder with my cricket bat in order to immobilise but not damage him. Should our Government publish an instruction pamphlet?

John Perriss
Hook Norton, Oxfordshire

SIR – As a Canadian watching this debate unfold in Great Britain, it seems to me that the great civility that defined the British Empire has drifted away in a cloud of idiotic, ultra-liberal influences.

Any good citizen of Britain of old knew what to do with burglars entering their home at night armed with twelve-inch knives: you simply shot them. Behold, crime was extremely low.

I grieve for you, Mother England, the land of my sires. Your country is a mess and only you can fix it.

T.B.
Toronto, Canada

BUM-BOMBERS

SIR – I was fascinated to learn that terrorists have taken to using their rectums as improvised explosive devices.

Apparently Abdullah Hassan al-Alseery (known to his pals as Ass) used his "Bum Bomb" in a failed attempt to kill a Saudi Prince.

Can anyone explain to me how troops, aircraft carriers, submarines, helicopters and airport security can defend us from exploding saucepans and ****holes?

Bring back Bomber 'Arris, I say.

David Mawson
Chesterfield, Derbyshire

SIR — "It's a wake-up call". That's what politicians say after every terrorist outrage. So who are these security experts who need to be woken up on a regular basis? Are they all teenagers who can't bear to get out of bed before three in the afternoon?

Jim Dawes
Maidstone, Kent

SIR — According to the *Telegraph,* a "chilling" threat was made by the Detroit bomber that "there are many more like me".

Forgive me if I remain unchilled. That there are many more deluded lame-brains I have no doubt, and for my part they are all welcome to set fire to their own legs.

J.M.
Walton-on-the-Naze, Essex

SIX MONTHS' HARD LABOUR

SIR – Surely Harriet Harman's plan to grant six months' paternity leave to fathers discriminates against those fathers unable to claim this benefit – such as unemployed youths who impregnate their unmarried girlfriends.

In the interests of equality I suggest that these people should be offered six months' hard work: this may even have a contraceptive effect.

L.M.
Staining, Lancashire

SIR – We have a very sad situation where it seems that all our clean-cut, disciplined youth are being sent to their deaths in Afghanistan while the unemployable hooligans and criminals are molly-coddled with free holidays, colour television and human rights defences.

Surely the simple answer is to send the thugs to Afghanistan, thereby killing two birds with one stone. And, who knows, those who survive will almost certainly come back the better for the experience.

B.C.
Somerset

SIR – Lord Harris has complained about the inordinate cost of keeping dangerous dogs impounded by the Metropolitan Police in kennels. A much more efficient use of resources would be to parachute them behind Taliban lines, preferably after several days' starvation.

Imagine the effect of 500 pitbulls descending from the heavens, furiously yapping and snarling.

Michael Marten
London W11

SUPER-OFFENSIVE CARS

SIR – The solution to the problem of illegally parked supercars belonging to foreign visitors to London is to have a council official drive round in a battered, reinforced ex-army Land Rover and "accidentally" graze the offending cars down one side.

The message would soon get round as to the fate of these freeloaders leaving expensive cars willy-nilly anywhere in the capital.

John Wain
Torquay, Devon

SIR — The solution to the illegal parking of supercars outside Harrods is, in my view, very simple: lift them up, put them in the compound and wait for the owner to collect them.

I was relieved when El Fahad (I don't even want to know how to spell it) sold Harrods and I thought I may even visit it for the first time, but now I'm not so sure.

I am well travelled, so have nothing against foreigners, but these spoilt brats have to learn a lesson or two.

R.B.
Somerset

THE WAREHOUSE AFTER THE NIGHT BEFORE

SIR — It is necessary to inconvenience those who cause the problem of binge-drinking. An out-of-town warehouse, with sexes segregated by Arris fencing, a recovery area with a doctor in attendance, where miscreants can be held in discomfort and under surveillance until at least 3pm the following day, should do the trick.

Lack of sleep, difficult transport home, a doctor's fee and the threat of criminal prosecution for abusive, threatening or violent behaviour — all this might make them regret the night before.

Robert Spratt
Upton St Leonards, Gloucestershire

SIR – Every major hospital should have a cold turkey room, with rubber walls, a sloping concrete floor and hosing-down facilities.

T.J. Tawney
Hildenborough, Kent

SIR – The current practice of taking drunks to Accident and Emergency only encourages them.

The answer is a night in a cold police cell, no blankets, followed by a mop and bucket in the morning to clean up any mess before appearing at the magistrates' court.

Graham Hamblin
Burton upon Trent, Staffordshire

UNHAPPY MEAL

SIR – If I go into a pub, already intoxicated, the landlord will refuse to serve me. Wouldn't it be a good idea if McDonald's, Burger King and other fast-food outlets were to adopt the same policy with the obese?

Robert Readman
Bournemouth, Dorset

LET SLIP THE DOGS OF NORTHUMBRIA

SIR — I was amazed at the amount of manpower, technology and weaponry used to capture Raoul Moat. Would bloodhounds not have done the trick?

Anthony Yannaghas
Bildeston, Suffolk

SIR — Should a Raoul Moat type incident arise in the future why don't the BBC and ITV interviewers combine to hunt the suspect, leaving the police to give the public regular inane reports throughout the day, interspersed with a few sly digs regarding the way the investigation is being conducted?

Norman Davies
New Milton, Hampshire

SIR — It beggars belief that the Northumbria Police Force took so long to find Raoul Moat.
    From my former experiences as a teenager, I reckon that a couple of troops of Boy Scouts would have found him within a day.

A.R. Hembrough
Disley, Cheshire

THE USE
AND ABUSE OF
LANGUAGE

I AM NOT YOUR MATE

SIR — My husband, mother-in-law and I, in our fifties and eighties, were recently addressed by young servers in a Buckinghamshire pub-restaurant as "You guys", which seemed to me to be inappropriate and unprofessional.

I have also been addressed on several occasions by workmen as "mate", even though I am obviously not a man.

Susan Tricklebank
Horton, Northamptonshire

SIR — Years and years ago, when I was a boy, when there were wolves in Wales, and birds the colour of red-flannel petticoats whisked past the harp-shaped hills, it was called *Saint* Valentine's Day.

Don Donovan
North Shore City, New Zealand

SIR — Surely I cannot be the only one who grimaces when someone replaces the simple phrase "in the future" with "going forward"? This one really grates.

Jeremy C.N. Price
Cross in Hand, East Sussex

SIR – I may well be the only one who is infuriated by the frequent misuse of the word *lead* to mean the past tense of *to lead*. It is *led*. I cannot *have lead*, unless it is in my pencil.

Lt Col D.E.C. Russell
Sherborne, Dorset

SIR – I notice with regret that the spoken name of the second month has been changed, almost universally, from *February* with its lovely rolled "r", to an uninteresting *Febuary*.

G.G.
Cheadle Hulme, Cheshire

SIR – When will more people stop saying *less* people rather than *fewer* people?

Chris Yates
Peasedown St John, Somerset

SIR – It is becoming almost mainstream for telephone operators to pronounce the "h" as "haitch" and it makes me cringe every time I hear it.

Richard Kinch
Aylesbury, Buckinghamshire

SIR — I've often wondered whether Britain's education system is in a state of decline. Then I visited Google and started to type, "Can I get...". Before I finished my query the first suggested search in the drop-down list appeared: "Can I get pregnant from a dog?"

Now I know.

Robin Whiting
Castle Rising, Norfolk

SIR — If the National Literacy Trust thinks that writing on Facebook, Twitter and the like is good for literacy they have obviously never actually read Facebook. The standard of spelling is absolutely atrocious.

Writing "literacy" as "litterassy" and calling that literate is somewhat akin to adding two and three and making seven and calling that numerate.

Dr John Gladstone
Gerrards Cross, Buckinghamshire

SIR — Why is it that language pedants are always *complete* a***holes?

Robert Dobson
Seal, Kent

STRUGGLES WITH WELSH

SIR – During the general election results in Wales examples of risible pronunciation, incorrect number and gender, erroneous lenition, and general discomfort in the native tongue were broadcast to the nation.

It is absolutely right that the returning officers should deliver the results bilingually, but those who struggle to express themselves in Welsh with anything less than consummate style, fluency and accuracy must realise that being near enough is not good enough.

It was the local government equivalent of Les Dawson playing Beethoven in the presence of Alfred Brendel.

David Davies
Bethesda, Gwynedd

I'M GONNA LEAD THE LABOUR PARTY

SIR — One wonders if the elocution tutor at Harriet Harman's elitist fee-paying school would have agreed that the persistent use of annoyingly sloppy diction, as in "Gonna", "Wanna" and "Shoulda", is an essential attribute for a Leader of the Opposition.

John Holland
Maidenhead, Berkshire

SIR — One must hope that David Miliband or Ed Balls is chosen as the next leader of the Labour Party. Their inability to pronounce the letter "t" and their tendency to form sentences without a verb should remind the electorate that not since 1997 have we had a prime minister who spoke the Queen's English in a faultless fashion.

Thank goodness we have one now who will, I am sure, cure his deputy of speaking like an excited teenager.

Roy Williams
Aberporth, Ceredigon

SIR – I was listening to Ed Balls this morning on the radio. Would it be possible to persuade the BBC to add a voiceover for those of us who only understand English?

Harry Fox
High Wycombe, Buckinghamshire

NO, THANK YOU VERY MUCH INDEED

SIR – Please can someone get the BBC's *Today* programme presenters, especially Evan Davis who seems particularly afflicted, to refrain from their irritating and time-wasting practice of thanking everyone, including their colleagues, "very much indeed"?

In most instances a simple "thank you" suffices. All my pleas to the *Today* website for them to desist have apparently been ignored.

Andrew Blake
Shalbourne, Wiltshire

SIR — I am becoming very tired of hearing people in supposedly intelligent conversation on Radio 4, and elsewhere, uttering "you know" (often *yeno*) after or even during every sentence.

If I did know, it is likely that I would not be listening to them.

Tim Field
Milborne Port, Dorset

MY SOLITARY WAR AGAINST THE BBC

SIR — While we wring our hands and moan about the standard of children's speech, it seems that the BBC is actively involved in promoting this demise. During last week's *Blue Peter* I counted over 30 occurrences of the dreaded glottal stop from the three presenters.

As a primary school teacher who is seemingly waging a solitary war against this insidious linguistic malaise, I wait to see whether future shows will include the two other main ingredients of chav-speak: the overuse of *amazin'*, and the omnipresent *like*, as in, "I'm like amazed, like, that the BBC, like, lets this kind of, like, stuff, go on, like."

As you may infer, I don't like it, like.

David Bulless
Cheltenham, Gloucestershire

SIR – Isn't it time that someone in the BBC gave John Humphrys a few basic lessons in pronunciation? Week after week he persists in saying *Tweny*. Surely after all his years as a journalist he knows that *twenty* has two "ts"? It sounds sloppy, especially in such an erudite programme as *Mastermind*.

Clare M. Blake
Sutton, Surrey

SIR – Why do broadcasters pronounce *kilometre* incorrectly? Doesn't anyone check up on them?

Mike Cole
Bridgwater, Somerset

SIR – I wonder if any of your readers would care to join in my campaign to ban television presenters from using the words *fantastic*, *amazing* and *incredible*. They would instead be allowed to say *boring*, *overblown* and *rubbish*.

Tim Nixon
Braunton, Devon

SIR – May I suggest that those media presenters who deliver travel news invest in a thesaurus. They would find that *treacherous* is not the only adjective which can be applied to roads in adverse weather conditions.

They may also learn that their reports are not only *uninformative*, but also *tedious*, *unimaginative*, *lifeless*, *prosaic* – and just plain *dull*.

R.G. Gavin
Cheltenham, Gloucestershire

SIR – Can someone please explain the difference between *local* showers and the *localised* ones to which weather forecasters increasingly refer?

Andrew Blake
Shalbourne, Wiltshire

SIR – I'd be happy if instead of sacking the Met Office, the BBC sacked its unintelligible female weather forecasters. They all speak through their noses and cannot pronounce vowels – I suppose this is why the ones on television use elaborate hand signs to get their message across.

Denise Hurst
Poole, Dorset

SIR – I am becoming increasingly annoyed by weather forecasters who insist on telling me how to dress and news reporters who talk of something that sounds like *hoppittals* rather than hospitals.

I suspect I am not alone.

John Wheeler
Easterton, Wiltshire

SIR – If I hear the words "true grit" again this winter, I think I'll throw up.

Clive Pilley
Westcliff-on-Sea, Essex

SIR – As a regular Radio 4 listener, I am dismayed by the growing number of (mostly female) correspondents, weather forecasters, programme guests and so forth who have "soppy" voices – halfway between a child's alto and an adolescent's soprano, with a wobbly twist added.

Is this the result of watching too many television cartoons in their formative years, or is it taught at school nowadays?

John McDermott
Montmorillon, France

SIR – Subtitles might be more accurate if newsreaders improved their enunciation. Then we would avoid rain for the next *40A Towers* and treatment on the *NA Chess*.

David Askew
Woking, Surrey

SCHOOL'S PET PAEDOPHILE

SIR – Your headline, "School paedophile checks for festive volunteers" caused me great concern. What kind of school has its own paedophile to check up on its festive volunteers? Is no one else available? I think that the public in general, and the parents of the children in that school in particular, have a right to know.

Alternatively, your proof readers need to pay more attention.

Philip Thomas
Poling, West Sussex

SIR – Headline on today's front page: "Spot checks on parents to catch school entry cheats".

Who's a clever dog?

John Winters
Wallingford, Oxfordshire

SIR – Has *The Daily Telegraph* started a "Most Mixed Metaphors" competition? In yesterday's paper a Met Office forecaster was quoted as saying, without so much as a "sic": "In these circumstances we need to sit around a table and look at the thresholds to see if they should be made more flexible."

And today, you write of the Chilcot inquiry: "[it] is unlikely to find the smoking gun that finally nails Mr Blair".

What a versatile weapon.

Elizabeth Jones
London SE10

SIR – I'm astonished at the elasticity of 21st-century youngsters. I read that the eight-year-old accuser in the trial reported today "sat on her hands all day and bit her fingers nervously".

Dr Barry Sturman-Mole
Newton Mearns, East Renfrewshire

SADDENED BY HACK PHRASES

SIR — Over the past couple of months I've noticed the emergence of the latest hack phrase: "to be left (with)". Thus "left with a broken heart"; "left defenceless"; "left running the family" etc.

A challenge to journalists: try working with the language instead of cliché, or leave me saddened by your laziness.

David Thomas
Ystradowen, Carmathenshire

SIR — At what age does a *toddler* become a *kiddie*? And is the next level of media-speak evolution a *loved* one?

Stephen Eeley
Oxford

SIR — When will the so-called "media", including *The Daily Telegraph*, restore adverbs and the pronoun whom?

R.A Last
South Croydon, Surrey

SIR – Where has this ubiquitous word "up" come from? It has now reached the front page of today's *Daily Telegraph*: "Free up cells".

Sally Browne
Westcliff-on-Sea, Essex

SIR – Good dictionaries still recognise that one who escapes is an *escaper*. Why then has the *escapee* crept into print?

I'm only an accountant, but I care about words too.

John Courtis FCA
Reydon, Suffolk

SIR – I am sure that I am not alone in deploring the regularly repeated misuse, in your usually meticulous newspaper, of the word *ultimate* for cruise ships' advertisements.

It means "last, final, beyond which no other exists or is possible".

There are few ultimate voyages on which I would wish to be a passenger.

Hugh Smorfitt
Tichborne, Hampshire

SIR – When was the last time the *Telegraph* appeared without a full-page cruise advert?

P.J.B.

SIR – To those that vent their frustration on the misuse of the English language I regret that it is time to draw stumps when this newspaper, which one would imagine to be a shining light in correctness, displays the headline in Saturday's Travel supplement: "Getting your APPS 2gether".

John Spiers
Bursledon, Hampshire

SIR – You should set an example and know better than to use the horrible phrase "chills out", instead of the proper English verb "relaxes".

"Chill out" is the ghastly slang of the African-American urban underclass, the last thing I expect to read in *The Daily Telegraph*.

Are you pandering to political correctness, like the lamentable BBC?

M.J.C.

STUFFING THE PARTRIDGE

SIR — I currently work for a wonderful company run by Americans. However, many of my British colleagues are beginning to find their business vernacular rather annoying: *step up to the plate; came in from left field; ball-park figure; circle the wagons; drink the Kool-Aid.*

We have taken a different approach to combat its pervasiveness: we have invented our own "Empire vernacular", which our American "co-workers" will believe is a quaint old English idiom.

Here are some examples we use regularly: *It's like trying to find the corner on a bowler hat; We can all sip sherry over this one; To hit the driven grouse would mean swinging across the line; and I'll stuff the partridge and get back to you.*

Our ultimate hope is that on global conference calls, we will one day hear these phrases spoken with an American accent.

E.B.
London SW6

NAMING THE NOUGHTIES

SIR — Am I alone in finding the word *Noughties* the most abhorrent manufactured word of the first decade of the 21st century?

Tony Skinner
Bourne End, Buckinghamshire

SIR – I'm not at all sure the term *Noughties* adequately reflects the decade. As things have turned out, perhaps *Owe-Owes* could be adopted.

Roger Fowle
Back Ends, Gloucestershire

SIR – Your article on words that define a decade was interesting and informative. But where were *chav*, *s**** and *f****? They may not often appear in written form but they are ubiquitous in the spoken language, and certainly define this country.

Reggie Byram
Elland, West Yorkshire

POLITICAL CORRECTNESS GONE BAD

SIR – Getting on for 50 years ago, I managed by the skin of my teeth to graduate from Oxford with what is now a degree of the past: a fourth. Don't knock it; lots of us managed to get one, and we regret their passing.

But what has happened to Oxford now? I am privileged to receive the alumni bulletin. Among the announcements of various dinners in New York, Shanghai and Hong Kong, the latest issue treats us to news of another upcoming event: The Gay and Lesbian Alumni Dinner.

What is this? Is it political correctness rearing its ugly head in the one place one might have hoped would rise above such a phenomenon?

Anthony Tucker
Tremons, France

SIR – You report that students have been taking heroin at an Oxford college. Truly a shock to the system. What with that and the buggery they'll probably all end up in the Lords.

J.D.
Chorley, Lancashire

SIR – Harriet Harman really doesn't need to worry her pretty little head over what a committee wishes to call its head. If the position is held by a woman who takes offence at the term "chairman", she will be quite capable of letting that be known by virtue of the position she holds.

C.W.U.
Redruth, Cornwall

PREPARING FOR BOYS

SIR — Seen on a school name board: "For Girls 8–18. Preparatory for Boys".

David Martin
Caterham, Surrey

SIR — Notice seen on the door of the Coventry Citizens' Advice Bureau today: "Due to Excessive demand we are closed for advice".

Paul Blundell
Coventry

SIR — I have just returned from a very pleasant day in London, marred only by two glaring spelling mistakes.

The first was not one but two identical printed posters as one enters The Royal Courts of Justice, saying that Trolley's (sic) were not permitted inside.

The second was a white metal sign in the middle of the road, pointing the way to ALDYWCH.

Joyce Chadwick
Stratford-upon-Avon

SIR — I recently had occasion to telephone the HM Revenue and Customs helpline to ascertain to which of two of their offices I should direct a particular tax form. I was politely informed that it really doesn't matter "because we've gone virtual".

Should I feel reassured by this, or just plain terrified?

Brian Adams
Swanbourne, Buckinghamshire

ATOMICALLY ATROCIOUS PUNS

SIR – Are nuclear families so called due to the tendency of one or other parent to go ballistic?

J.M.
Broadstone, Dorset

SIR – In light of the current weather is the Al Goreithm for global warming wrong?

A. Grant
Epsom, Surrey

SIR – With the England World Cup squad about to be announced a team song will surely follow. Presumably it will be sung A Capello.

C.C.
Swanage, Dorset

SIR – Now that Desmond Tutu has given such a warm and exuberant welcome to the inauguration of the 2010 football World Cup, can we expect him to be promoted to Archbishop Four-Nil?

J.D.
South Harting, West Sussex

SIR – As our Queen is one of the wealthiest people on the planet, why does she not buy Greece for Prince Philip and then call the country *Greek Britain*?

R.G.
Ringwood, Hampshire

SIR – Does the proposed plan to scrap police overtime mean a ban on copper nitrate?

R.W.
Mere, Wiltshire

SIR – I can't see the Kraft takeover of Cadbury working out. The two companies are like choc and cheese.

K.N.
Glasgow

SIR – Is a pay freeze an iced lolly?

> **L.W.**
> Minsted, West Sussex

SIR – With two thrusting young male leaders, do we now have a well-hung Parliament?

> **H.N.**
> Cailhavel, France

SIR – In view of his Dutch antecedents perhaps the media should consider referring to the new Deputy Prime Minister as Nick Clogg.

> **A.M.**
> The Hague, Netherlands

SIR – Perhaps the Labour party should make the younger Miliband and Mr Balls joint leaders on the grounds that two Eds are better than one.

> **M.S.**
> London SE23

SIR – No doubt a particular Labour Party vehicle will soon be gaining momentum. But will it be the Milibandwagon or the Milibandbandwagon?

> **D.P.**
> Stratford sub Castle, Wiltshire

SIR – Was the Ottoman Empire the first example of sofa government?

> **G.B.**
> Grassington, North Yorkshire

SIR – Susan Boyle's album may have reached number one, but Pope Benedict's will surely be the Christmas best-seller. After all, he's got the XVI factor.

> **W.M.S.**
> Norwich

SIR – I read with interest about the man who regularly makes love to cars. What a good thing he has not been indulging in similar practices with lorries. Otherwise he might have ended up HGV positive.

> **J.F.**
> Waiheke Island, New Zealand

SIR — If one puts a first-class stamp on a French letter, does it make the male come any quicker?

N.K.
Tilston, Cheshire

SIR — I read that Ms Winfrey is to launch her own TV network. Will it screen Soap Oprahs?

S.H.
Ardington, Oxfordshire

INDIANA BORIS AND THE LATIN CRUSADE

SIR — I am so thankful that both my daughters were taught Latin and Ancient Greek at school by inspiring teachers.

Boris Johnson might perhaps, for one day, forego the mountain bike and walk into work wearing a leather jacket and a broad-brim trilby hat, carrying a haversack and a coiled bull whip, and look around him and growl: "Anti-classicists? I *hate* anti-classicists."

Graham Clifton
Kingston upon Thames, Surrey

SIR – Ed Balls is an illogical arse. If Latin cannot inspire or motivate pupils, why are there any Latin teachers left at all? Could it be because they were inspired and motivated by their Latin teachers? Perhaps a classical education, with its emphasis on logic, reason and intellectual rigour, might have benefited the hapless politician.

If he still thinks that pupils don't enjoy their Latin lessons, he is more than welcome to visit the Barbarian Northern wilds and be proved hopelessly wrong.

Idiot.

Nick Witteveen (Head Of Classics)
Terrington Hall School, North Yorkshire

SIR – The good news is we may never see Ed Balls again because he'll be stuck in a cinema wondering what Exit means.

Robert Vincent
Wildhern, Hampshire

TRAVELLING THE ROADS TO HELL

NO-THRILLS AIRLINES

SIR – Am I alone in hating Ryanair more than the Taliban and liquorice combined?

Chris Sandilands
Carousel I, Stansted Airport

KEEPING BA'S COSTS – AND LUNCH – DOWN

SIR – I recently flew to New York with British Airways and was dismayed by what appeared to be an ingenious, yet fiendishly unscrupulous, ploy to keep its costs down.

Having taken off shortly after 8.20am we were immediately served lunch: a choice of chicken curry or lamb chops. The bemused cabin crew were unable to explain why lunch was being served for breakfast. I can only deduce that BA were hoping that passengers would lighten the craft's payload early in the flight.

Incidentally, the chicken curry was not spicy – something BA should re-examine. A pinch of chilli powder might bring even greater returns to its shareholders.

D.G.
London NW2

SIR – I propose that in the event of British Airways staff voting in favour of strike action, the airline should be re-branded "Air Lemming" in order to comply with trades description legislation.

Tom Caplin
Pulborough, West Sussex

SIR – Steve Turner of Unite says that his members will "have their say". I should inform him that, as one of a family of five who are long-standing BA executive club members, we are having our say and booking with Virgin Atlantic, whose staff earn considerably less and, some say, smile more.

Peter Sander
Hythe, Kent

COME SAIL WITH ME

SIR — Virgin is currently running an advertising campaign for its fly/cruise holidays using an attractive young lady dressed in a Merchant Navy officer's hat and little else.

Unfortunately, none of the ships featured is British registered, so this young lady does not have the right to wear our uniform, the wearing of which is protected under law.

However, all is not lost. If this young lady would like a berth in my British-flag container ship then she should report to my cabin forthwith.

Captain Peter J. Newton
Chellaston, Derbyshire

VOLCANIC SLICES

SIR — I have great sympathy for those air travellers thwarted by volcanic ash. I'm pretty certain it's not doing my golf much good either.

Roger H. Fowle
Chipping Campden, Gloucestershire

SIR – Last year it was cash; this year ash. Iceland sure makes a big mess for a small country.

Lester May
London NW1

SIR – Why not invade Iceland and fill that old volcano with reinforced concrete?

W.D. Harcourt
Ballymena, Co Antrim

SIR – Why not point all our wind farms towards the volcano and blow the ash back?

I.C. Elson
East Harling, Norfolk

SIR – Did anyone actually check the volcano? My guess is that it was surrounded by BA staff with coal fires and bellows, trying to get another few days off.

Emma Meader
Norwich

SIR – The last time this volcano erupted was in 1823. After that there were no flights for 80 years

Stanley Blaiwais
Salford, Lancashire

SIR – So, the "ban was unnecessary", was it?
Fine, next time this happens I suggest the situation
is tested by a plane-load of *Telegraph* journalists flying
into the ash cloud to ensure it's safe for the rest
of us.

J.M. Parsons
Sheffield

SIR – How long before your compiler includes this
damn volcano in *The Daily Telegraph* crossword?

Jeremy Brittain-Long
Constantine, Cornwall

SIR – Although it may outrage ardent feminists the
threat of Icelandic ash has galvanised me into action.
I've bought my wife a new set of dusters.

Robert Vincent
Wildhern, Hampshire

TORTURED COMMUTERS

SIR – Travelling by tube has become a living hell due to Transport for London's obsession with repetitive noise pollution. You know the stuff: all those dispiriting and pointless announcements they boom at us poor trapped passengers without respite.

TfL have told me to "please mind the gap between the train and the platform" more than 30,000 times. All right, all right! I know about the bloody gap! Please tell them to shut up about it.

This is serious. Repetitive noise pollution is recognised by the United Nations as a form of torture. It raises our blood pressure and shortens our lives. It must stop.

Barry Tighe
London E11

SIR – The EU states that a small calf transported by rail must be afforded a space of between 0.3 metres and 0.4 metres squared in which to travel.

I was wondering to whom I should write to complain about the fact that my feet didn't touch the floor for 45 minutes on the 15:44 to Sevenoaks from London Bridge last night.

S.B.
Sevenoaks, Kent

SIR — I'm the sort of person who would find something to complain about in heaven, but I am sure I am not the only commuter who is annoyed by the behaviour of "aisle jockeys". I do not understand why people insist on sitting on the outside seats when they know they will be disturbed by passengers joining the train further down the line.

When politely asked to make room for others their body language is invariably begrudging and sometimes openly hostile.

Clive Pilley
Westcliff-on-Sea, Essex

SIR — I see that St Pancras Station has been advertising extensively their "display of ice sculptures throughout December". At all other stations are these not known as "commuters"?

George Barker
Great Raveley, Cambridgeshire

SIR — Woman making a phone call on a recent 8.15pm train from Manchester to Macclesfield: "I'm in the quiet carriage."

James Greer
London SW16

SIR – As a traveller on the Tyneside Metro transport network I am uneasy when, before the working day has started, I see young women sitting in their seats applying their make-up. The process sometimes lasts the whole journey of over 20 minutes.

Graham Scott
Whitley Bay, North Tyneside

SIR – Railway travel used to be a pleasure. Now seats arc low, hard and sloped to dig into the small of your back. After travelling to Oxford and Birmingham last week, I was lame for half a day.

James Lewis
Wembley, Middlesex

SIR – No wonder society is crumbling. What have we come to when people cannot take responsibility for their own newspapers on trains?

N.D.
East Molesey, Surrey

PIG-IGNORANT
HEALTH AND SAFETY

SIR – On this morning's overcrowded Virgin train from Coventry to London, it was announced to the standing first-class passengers that, having paid £250 for a ticket, they could not take part in the breakfast service because of "health and safety".

Could any of your readers suggest techniques whereby a grown adult can eat a bacon roll served in a napkin while standing up without risking actual bodily harm to themselves and those around them?

Dr Jason Price
Barford, Warwickshire

SIR – 'elf and safety! Bah, humbug! Accidents are God's way of teaching us to be careful.

D. Eluard Parry
Ellesmere, Shropshire

SIR – Health and safety, where are you? The days of the usherette with a torch for finding one's seat in a darkened cinema are alas long gone. Could we have a return, please?

Pat Cleary
London SW3

PROTECTING CAMERON'S HANDLEBARS

SIR – I am a keen cyclist. I had a friend and colleague who was a keen cyclist. One notable difference between the two of us is that I wear a helmet whereas he did not. I am alive. He is not.

Despite this loss I do not advocate compulsory helmet wearing for adult cyclists.

I am, however, confused: why does David Cameron often have his helmet on his handlebars and not on his head?

Scott Lunn
Richmond, North Yorkshire

SIR – Now that every main road in the country is festooned with cycle tracks and speed humps it is time to consider further initiatives.

I'd like to suggest horse lanes. These can easily be justified on grounds of road safety, animal rights and environmental friendliness. In addition, horses can jump over potholes rather better than cars.

Simon Shneerson
Chorleywood, Hertfordshire

DAISY'S METHANE EMISSIONS

SIR — I am extremely concerned to hear that if I don't cut down my weekly car journey by five miles, I will be contributing towards global warming. I have spoken to Daisy, one of our cows, who has agreed not to fart tomorrow. Does this mean that I can drive with a clear conscience?

Gareth Jones
Horrabridge, Devon

SIR — In May this year I walked all 96 miles of the West Highland Way. On one night I had the unfortunate experience of sharing a tent with a vegetarian. The atmosphere in the tent quickly became almost unbearable due to his extraordinary level of methane emissions.

The world's population has increased by some 2.5 billion over the past 20 years, a sizeable number of them vegetarians.

Incidentally, this one dropped out of the walk after three days.

Alan Richardson
Auchenblae, Kincardineshire

PUBLIC INCONVENIENCE

SIR – Yesterday evening I witnessed an individual relieve himself on a London Underground train travelling towards Uxbridge. I did not actually see him point his John Thomas at the floor and urinate, but I smelt it and I heard it, along with the ensuing joke between him and his companion.

I complained to British Transport police, but they are seemingly unable to take action as I did not see the act in great detail. Taking a urine sample for DNA tests to nail the perpetrator conclusively apparently costs in the region of £100, while the fine for this type of offence is in the region of £80.

So what is the point?

Paul Teale
Twyford, Berkshire

SIR – "I was showing a tiny bit of breast, but is it any different to showing your arm or foot?" inquires one of your correspondents, who was ordered off a bus after feeding her baby.

Absolutely not, I assure this rational lady. And so I, too, will refrain from helpfully employing my male member to point out city highlights to tourists on the top deck of the bus, while my car is having a service next week.

What a strange world we live in.

Gavin Littaur
London NW4

THE COMPUTER EMPATHISES WITH YOUR DELAY

SIR – Can there be anything more meaningless than an automated voice issuing an apology, as in "First Capital Connect are sorry for the inconvenience caused"?

Does the computer feel remorse? I think not.

Alan Budd
Flitwick, Bedfordshire

SIR – Is anyone as annoyed as I am with the sustained upsurge in commuter train information? Not only are we told at every stop where the train is going and where it will stop, we are also informed of the total number of carriages and which carriage we're sitting in.

What next? The train driver's breakfast?

S. Bell
Bromley, Kent

THE CAR WAY IN FRONT

SIR — I'm fairly relieved that I don't own a Toyota with a defective accelerator. Mind you, I wasn't stricken with BSE, bird flu, swine flu, salmonella, foot and mouth disease or global warming infection either.

Charles Dingwall
Lyford, Oxfordshire

PAY-PER-VIEW AIRPORT SECURITY

SIR — How long before recordings of the new airport body scanners are available on adult pay-to-view television channels? And how long before those who monitor these x-rays start arriving at work in long scruffy raincoats?

Brian Christley
Abergele, Conwy

SIR — As a Christian Englishwoman fast
approaching the age of 60 I allow no one to view my
unclothed body, save doctors and my husband.

H.T.
Sale, Cheshire

SIR — If the new airport body scanners are so
intrusive, why not issue all passengers with Lycra
body suits similar to those worn on television's
Hole in the Wall?

Rupert Willoughby
Stratfield Mortimer, Berkshire

SIR — I don't have the slightest problem with my
body parts being scanned and shown on a screen for
some hapless security chap to scrutinise. Said parts
in my case are far too unremarkable to be of any
interest to anyone.

However, for passengers who fear ridicule and an
invasion of privacy, may I suggest that all security
personnel are also scanned and the photos
displayed as lifesize reproductions on the walls of
the airport.

That at least would prove a suitable diversion
during tedious queuing time.

Louise Broughton
Bowness on Windermere, Cumbria

SIR – The cost of the full body scanners to be installed at airports could surely be partly subsidised by the NHS. Each user, on request, could take back home to his GP a print-out of the results. I'm sure it would speed up many diagnoses.

Vic Nicholson
Stockton on Tees

COLOSTOMY TO DECLARE

SIR – I have a metallic artificial hip and a permanent colostomy. The proposed full-body scanner will detect both potentially suspicious objects. Would it not be easier, then, if there was the equivalent of an "anything to declare?" security queue? Perhaps a nurse could be on hand.

Dr David Saunders
Blackfield, Hampshire

SIR – Will it now be appropriate for all male passengers to pass through security with their manhood on full display to ensure there is nothing strapped thereto? This might save enormous time.

Brian H. Lait
Maroni, Cyprus

SIR – Three years ago, when clearing security at a provincial airport, I was asked by an official to remove my right shoe. Being an amputee and in a wheel chair, it was far easier for me to detach the whole leg and proffer it for examination. At which stage, the official decided it was unnecessary to inspect the shoe. This failed to make sense either then or now.

In my seventies, the only effect of the incident was a boost to my morale because an airport official had considered me to look dangerous.

Raymond Barry
Laytham, East Yorkshire

RADICAL RACIAL PROFILING

SIR – This is a brilliant and simple solution to the controversy over racial profiling. All passengers will be required to step into a booth that scans for explosive devices and automatically detonates any device found. Harmless individuals will be released immediately after being scanned. Muffled explosions, contained within the booth, will be followed by an announcement that a seat has become available for standby passengers.

It's a win-win for everyone.

Robert Readman
Bournemouth, Dorset

EURO-NO-STARS

SIR – Why should we be surprised at the failure
of the train service through the Channel tunnel
over Christmas 2009? Surely we should have learnt
by now to suspect automatically anything that starts
with "Euro".

Richard Shaw
Dunstable, Bedfordshire

SIR – None of the problems with the Eurostar
trains would have occurred had the railway
company decided to stick with reliable and proven
steam traction instead of this new-fangled
electric nonsense.

John Eoin Douglas
Edinburgh

SIR – I am left wondering whether Eurostar is
dependent on wind turbines for its source of power.

Harry M. Randall
Cerne Abbas, Dorset

WELCOME TO LONDON CALAIS

SIR – Could we not start a campaign to have the next London airport outside Calais? Flat land, few people disturbed, quick and easy access from central London, helps European integration... I could go on and on.

David Teale
London W4

DEAR DAILY TELEGRAPH

DEAR PICTURE EDITOR

SIR — So far this week the *Telegraph* has carried only two photographs of property guru Kirstie Allsopp. Is your picture editor's infatuation with her coming to an end?

Ron Bendell
North Tawton, Devon

SIR — Is there any chance of a few more pictures of that nice Samantha Cameron in your paper? There were only a couple today, and only one in the Business section. Surely she should appear in the Sport section more often as well?

Jonathan Chappell
Kibworth Beauchamp, Leicestershire

SIR — I should imagine that almost all readers of *The Daily Telegraph* are perfectly aware of what Lord Mandelson, First Secretary of State, Secretary of State for Business, blah, blah, blah, looks like. So why waste valuable space publishing such an indecently sized photograph of him?

Roy Edwards
Woking, Surrey

SIR – As I pencilled in a moustache on your photograph of Lord Mandelson I wondered how many other readers were doing the same thing.

And is that fist his, or does it belong to somebody else?

John Knight
Bisley, Surrey

SIR – When can we have more pictures of Kirsty Young?

David Townson
Isleworth, Middlesex

SIR – Why does a newspaper of your quality devote so many column inches to a ditz like Joanna Lumley? This wrinkled, past-it actress gets far too much attention considering the daft opinions she holds.

Some of the best stuff Lumley ever did was without her clothes in her early films.

Bill McCall
New South Wales, Australia

SIR – That's twice in the last few weeks that you have put a picture of Joanna Lumley on your front page; keep up the good work.

P. C-G
Aberdeen

SIR – It is a sad day when such former beauties as Elizabeth Taylor and Brigitte Bardot only attract interest on your Science page.

Stephen Ennis
Thames Ditton, Surrey

THE DEPRESSING TELEGRAPH

SIR – Almost the only piece of news I could read in the paper today without feeling thoroughly depressed was the report of Elgar's attempt to play the trombone.

The rest appeared to be concerned with flagellation, mistresses, sex sprays, call girls, paedophiles, murderers, frauds and vampires – including a picture of some woman on page 34 displaying her bottom with gay abandon.

Christine Jones
Corwen, Denbighshire

SIR – One tries to remain loyal to the dear old *Telegraph*, even when it cross-dresses to attract *Guardianista* fops to swell its readership. But for the sake of your reputation as a newspaper of record I beg you to hire journalists who can tell handouts and government propaganda from genuine research in the field of climate-change baloney.

J.B.
Bridge of Weir, Renfrewshire

SIR – If you feed a cat it thinks it is God; if you read the *Guardian* you think you are intelligent; if you've got any sense you read the *Telegraph* and keep a dog.

Jonathan Goodall
Bath

AM I BOVVERED?

SIR – So Scarlett Johansson is having dinner with President Obama. Well, whoopee. To quote Catherine Tate: "Am I bovvered?"

David Butcher
Andover, Hampshire

SIR – Can anyone, anywhere, offer me the hope that one day I will open a newspaper and find no mention of the Bloomsbury set, the Amises, the Waughs and assorted luvvies giving awards to other luvvies?

Kerrie Howes
Brecon, Powys

SIR – Of the 40 people named in the 30 photographs on the *Telegraph's* "Celebrity Sighting" web page, I have heard of only 15 of them. I strongly suspect that many other readers would know even fewer.

May I suggest you change the page name to "Who?".

Robert Warner
Aston, Oxfordshire

SIR – Could someone please restrain the foot fetishist at *The Daily Telegraph* who cannot keep his or her eyes off the shoes of the new Home Secretary and find them a more useful purpose in life?

Peter Yarwood
Gresford, Clwyd

SIR — Was today really such a slow news day that you decided to give three-quarters of your front page over to cod-psychological nonsense brought on by the albeit untimely, and possibly sad, death of a minor contributor to something as fleetingly daft as "fashion"?

I understand that the death of "Lee" [sic] Alexander McQueen could be seen as a major event in the shallow world of fashion. To credit his life and achievements via your obituary columns would be decent and fair. However, to express such an amount of emotion over a chap who simply designed a few frocks is, as modern speech has it, simply OTT.

Claire Bellis
Co Meath, Ireland

SIR — Where were you when Nelson Mandela was released? I can't remember. Where were you when Alexander McQueen killed himself? I cried for an hour.

W.B.
Bangor, Co Down

SIR – I have long wondered if the stick-insect-like creatures who appear with regularity in the columns of this newspaper are indeed humans, or if the fashion shows of the world are a cover for alien species to visit the planet and meet up with their leaders – fashion journalists. Proof finally came on Saturday when one of the aliens carelessly allowed herself (itself?) to be photographed with her mini flying saucer attached to her head.

G.W.
Hemingford Grey, Cambridgeshire

SIR – At last one of your columnists has the spunk to record that so-called fashion parades are a nonsense. Also, why on earth do the "models" walk as if they are recovering from knee operations?

Alan Caville
Iteuil, France

TROUBLE UP T'WAITROSE

SIR – It's all very well cosying up to Waitrose, but what about us poor readers in t'north, where Waitrose is not represented? Can you not form an alliance with a pie maker up here so that we, too, can enjoy tasty spin-off benefits of readership?

P.R.
Ramsbottom, Lancashire

SIR (and you must be a man to be so cruel) – You have been teasing me all week in *The Daily Telegraph* with the promise of chocolate truffles. Today I was in Abingdon, early as usual, to do my weekly shop at Waitrose. I searched the paper for the coupon to tear out and, to my horror, on the reverse of the coupon was the crossword.

I left the store truffleless. Please don't do this again as it is bad for my blood pressure.

Christine Turley
Drayton, Oxfordshire

CROSS WORDS

SIR – For 60 years I have been doing the Saturday crossword, always on the back page, along with other important matters like the weather.

This morning my world was turned upside down as I stared uncomprehendingly at an advertisement for iPhone 3G, whatever that is.

I suppose a lucrative offer was made, but is nothing sacred any more?

Wg Cdr N.A.D. Nugent RAF (retd)
Hindhead, Surrey

SIR – FERCRISAKE! Are you barking mad? Moving the sacred crossword off the back page? What next? Tabloid format?

I've had to call my doctor for a sedative; this is worse than global warming, WMD, Chernobyl and the *X Factor* combined.

Please don't move the crossword off the back page.

Frank Hall
Ramsgate, Kent

SIR – I need to remove an annoying, full-page advert which has been placed where my crossword should be. Is there an app for that?

Steve Vaughan
Abingdon, Oxfordshire

NEVER MIND THE *******S

SIR – While I appreciate the desire to protect your readers' sensibilities by deleting most of the expletives that appear in your pages, could you not leave just one or two letters in place to give us a clue to the missing word(s), thus preventing a lot of frustration to some of your readers?

Ken Robson
Chatteris, Cambridgeshire

DEAR BRYONY GORDON

SIR — I was distressed to read that the fair damsel Byrony Gordon struggled to find a lunchtime companion. Please pass on my regards and tell her that if a slightly overweight, middle-aged and balding sales manager with an opinion on everything would make her lunchtime complete I am available at short notice.

Phil Cox
West Moors, Dorset

SIR — Bryony, I enjoy your column more than any other, because you make me smile. *The Daily Telegraph* wouldn't be the same without you. And please don't worry about the size of your jeans.

Charles Ranald
Itchen Stoke, Hampshire

SIR — May I ask where Bryony Gordon holidays? I would like to share her enjoyment of topless sunbathing.

P C-G
Aberdeen

SIR – As a leg-man of some standing I wonder why, in a paper that often limits the pictures of men to head and shoulders only, we're treated to so alluring and lengthy a bum/bosomy image of Bryony Gordon.

But why stop short at the legs? Is something amiss in this department perhaps? Are we talking plumpers, surgical stockings and the like? Or are her legs so magnificently turned as to distract attention from the paper?

Go on, give us a treat: let's have the full shout.

J.G. Dawson
Chorley, Lancashire

BUSINESS BILLIARDS

SIR – I see that all the top male business columnists are shown hand-in-pocket. At one time, this was regarded as the epitome of slovenliness. I also recall from my schooldays that it was referred to as "playing pocket billiards".

Mike Kelly
Belton, Leicestershire

DEAR AUNTIE HEFF

SIR — Given the demeaning descriptions, such as "little George", that Simon Heffer increasingly uses when describing members of the Conservative front bench, I presume he will have no objection to people using his own renowned nickname of "Auntie Heff".

Rodney Enderby
London N14

SIR — The therapeutic effect I experience from reading Simon Heffer's column on Saturday is worth my subscription in itself. And I have a dream: I dream that the readers of *The Daily Telegraph* unite and provide him with a white steed, a suit of shining armour and a mighty sword, then point him in the direction of Westminster to rid us of the "miserable drones and traitors we have nourished and brought up in our household".

Michael R. Greenway
Old Buckenham, Norfolk

THE INFLAMMATORY TELEGRAPH

SIR – While I would not consider the content of *The Daily Telegraph* especially inflammatory, I do depend on its substance being such when it comes to lighting fires.

Recently I've noticed that it is becoming increasingly difficult to ignite the paper in the normal fashion. Is this due to a hidden health and safety feature?

Andrew Klusaitis
Cookhill, Warwickshire

SIR – May I congratulate *The Daily Telegraph* on retaining its broadsheet style. I am doing some decorating at home and realise that it is now the only paper whose double sheets fit properly beneath a door to protect the floor while painting.

Ted Shorter
Hildenborough, Kent

SIR – A newspaper often leads a second life as fish and chip wrapping or as lining for the budgie's cage. But yesterday's outer advertising page is far more valuable: a double broadsheet of fine greaseproof paper with scant print –

perfect for wrapping cheese, or for children to trace on to.

I hope it will become a regular feature.

Stephen Phillips
London SE24

LETTERS THERAPY

SIR — Although my letters are not printed, I do thank you for the opportunity to beef off occasionally. It is very therapeutic.

Pat Cullen
Wincanton, Somerset

SIR — Most of my pub customers seem to read your letters page. So I thought I'd say that Rocky, the pub dog for 13 years, has died.

Ian Lewis
Alciston, East Sussex

SIR — If I have a letter printed in the *Telegraph* before the end of the year I stand to gain £1.50.

Unfortunately, I am neither wise nor witty but I am, perhaps, just a little bit wily.

Please print my letter.

Barbara Beattie
Neston, Cheshire

SIR – I was reminded by your article on letter-writers that about 20 years ago you published several letters from a dear friend of mine, Oscar Campion-Fenn.

You were almost certainly not aware that Oscar was a cat, and that the letters were authored by the man whom he owned, David Fenn.

Sadly, neither Oscar nor David are still with us to add spice to your letters page.

Simon Thorpe
Tetsworth, Oxfordshire

SIR – I am standing for UKIP as a parliamentary candidate and could do with some publicity. I have written hundreds of letters to the *Telegraph*, many of which have been published. I would appreciate it if you could do a piece on me as "A Man of Letters".

Anon

SIR – Thank you for publishing my letter today. I wonder if you would be good enough to publish this one too. I could then join in (and probably kill off) dinner party conversations with an opening: "Speaking as a regular contributor to *The Daily Telegraph*..."

M.R. Stallion
Braintree, Essex

SIR – My congratulations to Ann Salmon on joining our illustrious band of those who have had letters published by *The Daily Telegraph*. This will be talked about for a long time at dinner parties and will firmly put West Chiltington on the map.

Writing to *The Daily Telegraph* is a worthwhile career and the sense of achievement when your name stares back at you is superb. Just think of those whose names have never appeared: Barack Obama, Elvis Presley, David Beckham and Willy Wonka, to name but a few.

To reward this success and generate more envy in our neighbouring village, I ask *The Daily Telegraph* to create a special badge honouring the effort and persistence of its letter-writers.

Trevor Jones
West Chiltington, Sussex

SIR – I tried yesterday to explain to a class of 12 year olds the nuances of Letters to the Editor. One looked terribly confused for a moment before declaring: "Oh, I get it. It's like Facebook, but for intellectuals."

Chris Sparrow
Oxford

SIR – The picture featured on the letters page has charm and interest, and I now quite warm to it. So, do continue.

However, I suspect that it conceals where my own occasional letter to the editor would appear – now consigned perhaps to the *Am I Alone … ?* publication.

James Gibson
Quorn, Leicestershire

SIR – When I took up residence here some 20 years ago a letter I wrote to "the other paper" prompted a call from the lawyer handling my affairs to say that the senior partner in his first job had once said: "Never take on a client who writes letters to newspapers. They have too much time on their hands."

Denis Harvey-Kelly
Sherborne, Dorset

DEAR COWARDLY MISOGYNISTS ON THE LETTERS DESK

SIR – Why are you so reluctant to publish age-old, basic commonsense? Are you afraid of offending the great and the good, the Hampstead-dwelling, cappuccino-drinking, *Guardian*-reading elite?

My collection of letters the *Telegraph* refused to publish is nearly complete. Be warned!

> Yours, as always disgustedly,
> **M.D.**
> Harrow on the Hill, Middlesex

SIR – I note that in today's paper only three of the 22 letters are written by women. Do men possess better communication skills, write in a manner which is more likely to appeal to your editor, or is it possible that they have more time to hone their missives?

> Yours, in haste, between cooking and
> washing up supper,
> **Gillian Ellis**
> Oakwood, West Sussex

SIR – How did Graham Senior-Milne manage it?
A letter in *The Sunday Telegraph*, and another the
following day in *The Daily Telegraph*. What is his secret?
Is it the double-barrelled name? Is it the
Northumbrian address?

I have been trying for years now, much to the
amusement of my wife, to get a letter published in
either paper but without success, and the man from
Norham, Northumberland, manages two in two
days.

I am speechless.

> Disgusted of Tunbridge Wells
> **aka John M. McLennan**
> Coventry

HOLD THE FRONT PAGE

SIR – I have written a book, Bridget Jones style, but
the difference is that this book allows for the
spiritual progress that the protagonists need to make.

It is written with hilarity, but the final chapters
discuss the world situation.

This is a book for our times and will make a
brilliant film script.

If you are interested in serialising you may just
have the next sensation on your hands.

Please let me know and I will send you a sample.

> **S.D.**
> Ledbury, Hertfordshire

SIR – Good afternoon! I am a teacher of English language from Russia, Ekaterinburg. My name is Tatiana, my surname is Vaganova. My address is Russia. I want to publish my novel *Tears of Happiness* in your edition.

Thank you.

Tatiana Vaganova
Russia

SIR – I felt compelled to write to you with regard to moral standards at my old school and how they have slipped away.

I understand that there is an ongoing affair between a member of the management team and a female member of the games department. I find this sort of thing disgusting at the best of times, let alone when it's carrying on in such a grand place and the fact that it could be seen by the children attending. The morals of the two people concerned can't be much more than that of an alley cat.

In my time there this sort of thing would have been frowned upon.

A very concerned Old Boy

DEAR LADY WHOSE LIFE
I CHANGED

SIR — I wish to apologise wholeheartedly to the young lady I misinformed on Crewkerne railway station last Tuesday, sending her off to Plymouth rather than her intended destination of London.

It was only after she clambered aboard that I realised my terrible mistake. By, "Is that the London train?" she had, of course, meant was it going to London, not whether that was its provenance.

By my thoughtlessness I may well have altered the course not just of her day but, possibly, her entire life. I am very sorry.

Martin Roundell Greene
Henley, Somerset

THE DAILY DEATH

SIR — I buy the *Telegraph* every day. Not for your editorial content, nor for your news. No, merely because you still have the only reasonably comprehensive list of deaths.

C.H.
Salisbury

SIR – For me, a better read than the deaths on your Court and Social Page is the delightfully mellifluous "Appointments in the Clergy" with place names such as: "Peopleton and White Ladies Aston with Churchill and Spetchley and Upton Snodsbury and Broughton Hackett"; "Ticknall Smisby and Stanton by Bridge"; "Orlestone with Snave and Ruckinge"; "Patching St John".

If I were a poet, such names would be my inspiration. Sadly, I am not.

Peter Hiley
Poole, Dorset

SIR – Of the 59 deaths recorded in Wednesday's *Telegraph*, 39 stated the age of the deceased. Sixty-six per cent were over 80 and a remarkable 44 per cent over 90. If this shows that reading the *Telegraph* contributes to one's longevity then I'm going to take it regularly.

Colin Reeves-Smith
Purley, Surrey

P.S.

My dear Hollingshead,

Thank you for your letter regarding your new book.
You may certainly use my material but be aware that
you are introducing a sea-change in the way in which
people write to newspapers. For countless
correspondents, myself included, you now present a
dilemma — how to compose a letter that is not
memorable enough to make the columns of the daily,
yet may nevertheless be worthy of inclusion in an
annual compilation.

That, sir, is moving the bar to a fresh height.
While many will undoubtedly fall by the wayside,
there are some stalwarts, the undersigned among
them, who will match this with stoicism and redouble
— nay! *retreble* — our chunterings to your editor in the
blind, scatter-gun belief that, one way or another, we
will hit a bull's eye.

Arthur W.J.G. Ord-Hume
Guildford, Surrey